"Christina's expertise and proven track record helping children learn to identify and manage their emotions radiate throughout her new workbook. Her descriptions are thoughtful and concise. The variety of activities engages and appeals to all types of learners. This workbook is an easy-to-use tool for parents and clinicians to help the children in their lives learn to manage their emotions."

—**Amy Robinson**, mental health professional, board-certified behavior analyst, and doctoral student in school psychology

"*The Anger Workbook for Kids* provides appropriate language for children to understand their experiences of anger, and ways to manage it differently. Parents, go through this workbook with your child, and you can explore your own emotional responses and learn some strategies along with your child."

—**Jayme Baden, MA, LMFT**, community family therapist, and mother of three children

"*The Anger Workbook for Kids* provides kids (with the assistance of an adult) effective tools to manage the actions associated with poor anger management. Kids learn how to identify their feelings and triggers, and how anger can negatively affect their relationships with friends and family. The easy-to-use activities encourage kids to practice working through their feelings and controlling their actions. This workbook is useful for professionals and parents alike!"

—**Stacy Wilson, LCSW**, licensed clinical social worker and consultant providing cognitive behavioral therapy (CBT) to teens and adults

"If you are looking for kid-friendly approaches to managing anger, this book is a must-have. The exercises work well as self-guided practice for children and adolescents, or as a complement to therapy interventions. I love how complex emotional concepts are broken down in ways that kids and their caregivers will easily understand. I will return to it frequently in my work with youth in foster care."

—Amy Board, MSW, LCSW, director of community mental health at Little City Foundation

"This informative workbook is a hands-on tool that empowers children to identify, control, and manage the source of their anger. The easy-to-read information and interactive activities in this book make it an ideal resource for parents and/or other adults to use to help the children in their lives. This is a must-read book for anyone with children who may be displaying signs of anger."

—Kristin Mayer, master of arts in instruction and reading (WI 316), and 2nd grade teacher at Galesville Elementary School in Galesville, WI

"What a great workbook to help therapists and parents support kids who are coping with big feelings. This is even more crucial in this time as school is disrupted, and children and families are under unprecedented stress. Christina Kress normalizes anger and provides so many tools that you are sure to find some that work for your child. If you are looking for a road map to help kids understand and manage their feelings, this is it."

—Susan Nightingale, LICSW, vice president of mental health services at SOME (So Others Might Eat) in Washington, DC

The Anger Workbook for Kids

Fun DBT Activities to Help You Deal with Big Feelings & Get Along with Others

Christina Kress, MSW, LICSW

Instant Help Books
An Imprint of New Harbinger Publications, Inc.

Publisher's Note

This publication is designed to provide accurate and authoritative information in regard to the subject matter covered. It is sold with the understanding that the publisher is not engaged in rendering psychological, financial, legal, or other professional services. If expert assistance or counseling is needed, the services of a competent professional should be sought.

INSTANT HELP, the Clock Logo, and NEW HARBINGER are trademarks of New Harbinger Publications, Inc.

Distributed in Canada by Raincoast Books

Cover design and anger monster illustration by Sara Christian.

Illustrations on pages 29, 36, 49, 51, 61, 86, and 96 by Katie Sparks.

Interior book design by Amy Shoup.

Acquired by Elizabeth Hollis Hansen

Edited by Karen Schader

Library of Congress Cataloging-in-Publication Data

Names: Kress, Christina L., author.
Title: The anger workbook for kids / Christina Kress.
Description: Oakland, CA : Instant Help Books, [2021]
Identifiers: LCCN 2021000477 | ISBN 9781684037278 (trade paperback)
Subjects: LCSH: Anger in children--Juvenile literature. | Anger--Juvenile literature. | Stress management for children--Juvenile literature.
Classification: LCC BF723.A4 K74 2021 | DDC 155.4/1247--dc23
LC record available at https://lccn.loc.gov/2021000477

Printed in the United States of America

23   22   21

10 9 8 7 6 5 4 3 2 1   First Printing

To my clients, who have taught me so much

Contents

SECTION 3: Anger Can Hurt Others

SECTION 4: Pushing Back Against Anger

A Note to Parents

Emotions are complex and difficult to understand. Human beings do not come into this world understanding what their feelings are and how to manage them. Children depend on the adults around them to learn how to regulate and manage emotions through modeling, practice, and support. As infants, we cry when we're distressed, and adults soothe us from the outside in. As toddlers, we face shifting expectations; adults start to let us struggle a little more with our feelings, offering support as needed, but also expect us to experience difficult feelings and learn how to recover. This shift does not come easily to everyone for a variety of reasons. You may have a child in your life who, for whatever reason, needs some additional help from the adults around them with learning to manage their feelings, specifically anger.

The activities in this book were created by combining cognitive behavioral therapy with dialectical behavioral therapy (DBT). DBT is a treatment approach researched and developed by Dr. Marsha Linehan that is used with adults and adolescents who struggle with experiencing intense feelings. I have taken my years of experience working with children and combined it with my training and experience teaching DBT and created these activities to help kids who need to focus specifically on anger. I have used these activities in my sessions with kids to help them gain understanding and control of their anger or intense emotions.

I find that children learn best through experience, practice, and modeling by the adults in their life. Activities throughout this book are written directly to the child. Young children who struggle with anger can at times be frightened by the intensity of their own anger. Having an adult assist in learning to manage anger is crucial. I encourage you to keep this in mind as you work through the activities in this book. These activities are meant to be done alongside an adult and to build upon each other. At https://www.newharbinger.com/47278, you'll find supplemental material available for download. Your child may need help accessing this material.

It is my intention that you will use these activities as an opportunity for open communication and discussion with your child. I encourage you to use them as conversation starters to learn more about your child and their experience of anger. If the child you are working with requires a little flexibility in the activities in order to understand the concept being taught, I encourage you to feel free to make them more effective.

Remember that learning alone does not lead to behavior change. *Practice* leads to behavior change. Practice and repeat the activities as you see fit. As with any new skill, it takes practicing over and over to learn a new behavior.

Feelings and Thoughts

You have a lot of different thoughts and feelings throughout each day. Your day can start out great and end terrible depending on what happens around you and the thoughts and feelings you have along the way. This section will focus on reviewing the basic feelings you have from time to time and different types of thoughts that come along with them. Learning to work with feelings is hard and at times takes the help of an adult you trust. Think of the adults in your life that you trust and feel free to ask them for guidance.

ACTIVITY 1

Identifying Feelings

FOR YOU TO KNOW

Feelings and emotions are always changing. Notice that the word "emotion" actually has the word "motion" in it!

Feelings are reactions to things that happen around us. These reactions start in our body and brain, and we use feeling words to describe our experience. For example, your brother pushes you down. Your jaw becomes tight and your heart beats faster, telling your brain something is wrong. You are mad and you say, *"Stop!"*

Because our days are always changing, our feelings are always changing. We can have more than one feeling at a time, and feelings come in different intensities, or sizes. The more you get to know your feelings, the more you'll be able to learn about yourself and the better you'll be at handling your feelings as they come up.

FOR YOU TO DO

Read the story on the next page, and then answer the questions that follow to practice identifying the feelings in the story. This will be a good way to notice which feelings you have a hard time understanding and may need to learn more about.

Taylor woke up smiling from ear to ear! She knew today was going to be a great day. It was her birthday, and she had planned a great party. Taylor had invited all the people who were close to her: her friends from school, her grandparents, and her aunts and uncles.

Taylor's dad was helping set up for the party. They were having a bouncy house and carnival games in the backyard. When Taylor got downstairs, she noticed that the bouncy house was already set up and that her little brother was playing inside it. She did not want him ruining her party by hanging around and being annoying. Plus, if anyone should be trying out the games, it should be her, not her brother.

Taylor ran over to the bouncy house and knocked her brother down, yelling, "Get out of here! It's my party, and I don't want you around!" Of course, she got in trouble because he started crying like a baby. Her dad reminded her that at her brother's birthday party the month before, he had let her try the games before his guests arrived, and he probably thought she would do the same. Taylor thought about this and remembered it was true. She felt bad about what she had said and decided to go check on how her mom was doing with setting up inside.

Taylor's mom was busy setting up the darts and balloon games. When Taylor walked in, her mom told her that her friend Megan was not going to be able to make it to the party. This upset Taylor because Megan was her closest friend. Taylor began to feel uneasy, and she said to her mom, "What happens if more people call and say they can't come? What if no one comes to my party and I don't have any friends here for my birthday?" Taylor's mom reminded her that all the other people she had invited had said they were coming, and some had even called to make sure they knew the address. This reminder helped Taylor feel better.

The party was a huge success! A lot of people were there, everyone had fun playing games, and Taylor got some really exciting presents. When the day was over, she actually felt a little down because all the fun was over and she had to wait a whole year until her next birthday party.

FOR YOU TO DO

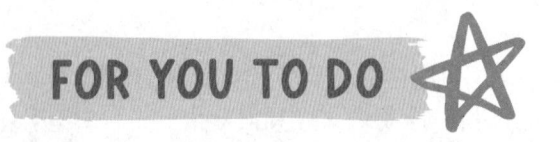

Answer the questions to practice identifying the feelings from the story. Use the feeling words listed in the word bank to help you. Hint: Remember that we can have more than one feeling at one time.

Word Bank

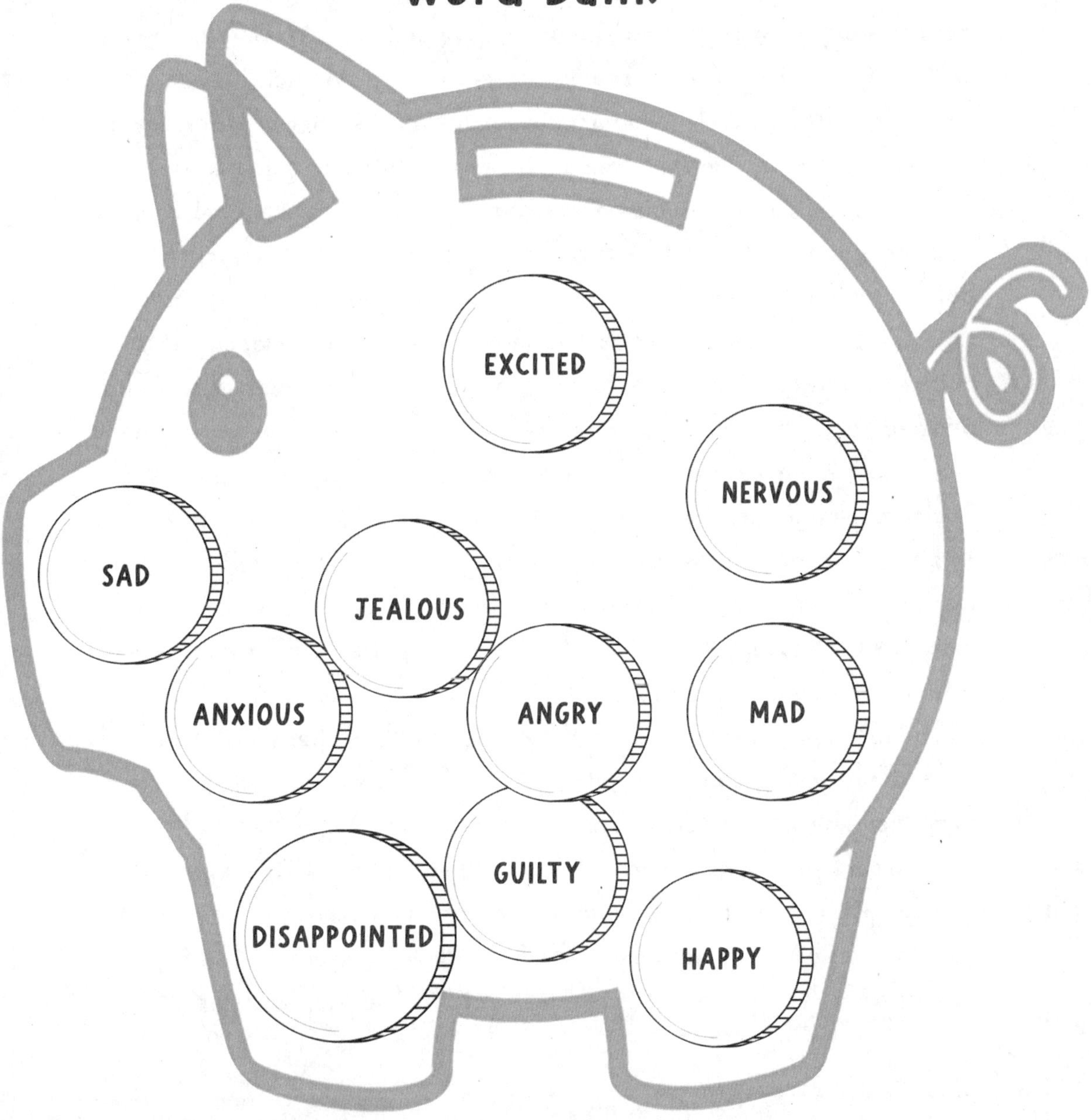

EXCITED
NERVOUS
SAD
JEALOUS
ANXIOUS
ANGRY
MAD
GUILTY
DISAPPOINTED
HAPPY

1. How did Taylor feel when she first woke up in the morning?

_____

2. What was Taylor feeling when she thought about all the special people who were coming to her party?

_____

3. How do you think Taylor felt when she found out her friend Megan could not come?

_____

4. How was Taylor feeling when she saw her brother in the bouncy house?

_____

5. What feeling did Taylor have after she pushed her brother down and then her dad reminded her that he had let her try the games at his party?

_____

6. Taylor was thinking about the "what-ifs" of people not coming to her party. What do you think she was feeling at the time?

_____

7. Once everyone went home, all Taylor could think of was the fact that the party was over. How do you think she was feeling?

_____

(See Appendix D for answers.)

ACTIVITY 2

What Causes Your Feelings?

FOR YOU TO KNOW

Your brain and body talk to each other and work as a team to manage and control your feelings.

When events happen around us or to us, our brain receives the message and tells our body how to react. Our brain and body work together to help us manage our feelings. Sometimes it's easier to identify feelings in other people than in ourselves. It is important to become more familiar with what types of events cause you to have certain feelings. Knowing this will help you feel more confident and in control when you have big feelings.

FOR YOU TO DO

Fill in this chart to practice identifying situations that would lead to you having certain feelings and recognizing how your body reacts to those feelings. One example has already been done for you.

FEELING NAME	WHAT CAUSES THE FEELING	HOW MY BODY REACTS
EXAMPLE: ANGER	My brother sneaks into my room and takes my iPad without asking.	Face hot, screaming, tight fists
ANXIETY/FEAR/ WORRY		
SADNESS		
HAPPINESS/JOY		
ANGER		

ACTIVITY 3

Big Feelings, Little Feelings

FOR YOU TO KNOW

No matter the size of your feelings, with practice, you can learn to stay in control of your actions.

Feelings come in different sizes. Sometimes feelings are big and strong, and last a long time. Sometimes feelings are small and pass quickly. Each time you have a feeling, it might be different. This can be confusing! To make things even more confusing, people in the same situation can have different feelings. You and a friend might go through the same experience and you would feel anger at a 10 but your friend would only feel anger at a 5. This is normal; people react in different ways.

FOR YOU TO DO

Read the situations on the next page and indicate what feeling you'd have and how big, or intense, it would be. Use the feeling scale to help you choose an intensity from 1 to 10. Then, ask at least two other people how they would feel and how big their feeling would be. Write down what they say. Notice how different everyone's answers might be.

You can also try this activity with more people, go to http://www.newharbinger. com/47278 and download a copy of this survey. If you need help, ask an adult.

1	5	10
VERY SMALL	FEELS STRONG BUT I CAN STILL HANDLE IT	BIGGEST IT'S EVER BEEN. I CAN'T STAND IT!

1	2	3	4	5	6	7	8	9	10

SITUATION #1	ME	PERSON #1	PERSON #2
YOU HAVE TO GET UP IN FRONT OF CLASS TO GIVE A PRESENTATION. YOU ARE SO NERVOUS THAT YOU JUST STAND THERE AND SAY NOTHING. THE WHOLE CLASS BEGINS TO LAUGH AT YOU.	FEELING: _____ INTENSITY: _____	FEELING: _____ INTENSITY: _____	FEELING: _____ INTENSITY: _____

SITUATION #2	ME	PERSON #1	PERSON #2
YOU NOTICE THAT YOUR SISTER LEFT HER IPAD OUT ON THE KITCHEN TABLE. YOU DECIDE TO USE IT WITHOUT ASKING HER PERMISSION, AND THEN SHE WALKS IN AND SEES YOU USING IT.	FEELING: _____ INTENSITY: _____	FEELING: _____ INTENSITY: _____	FEELING: _____ INTENSITY: _____

SITUATION #3	ME	PERSON #1	PERSON #2
YOU STUDIED REALLY HARD FOR YOUR SPELLING TEST AND THINK THAT MAYBE YOU DID WELL. WHEN YOU GET YOUR GRADE BACK, IT IS A C.	FEELING: _____ INTENSITY: _____	FEELING: _____ INTENSITY: _____	FEELING: _____ INTENSITY: _____

ACTIVITY
4

Feelings Have Jobs

FOR YOU TO KNOW

Feelings are the same all over the world. Even if you don't speak the same language as someone else, you can still communicate feelings through facial expressions and body language.

Feelings start in our brain and body. We show them on our face and through our actions. Feelings have three jobs:

- Other people's feelings are messages to us that something is happening to them.

- Our feelings are messages that something is happening to us that we need to pay attention to.

- Our feelings send us messages about how to change our behavior or how to act.

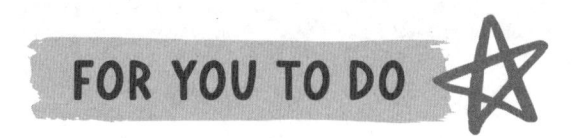

FOR YOU TO DO

Fill in the blanks to identify the different messages that emotions are communicating.

Imagine that you are in a classroom in China, and you don't speak Chinese. That would be a pretty difficult situation. Communicating with your classmates and teacher would be challenging. You share a table with a classmate named Ali.

Now imagine that a tiger walks into the classroom and is standing rightbehind you! You can't see the tiger because it's behind you, but Ali can see it.

Her brain reacts immediately, and her first thought is "A tiger! We have to _____!" Ali sees the tiger and feels _____

_____!

You hear Ali scream and look at her face, which looks like this:

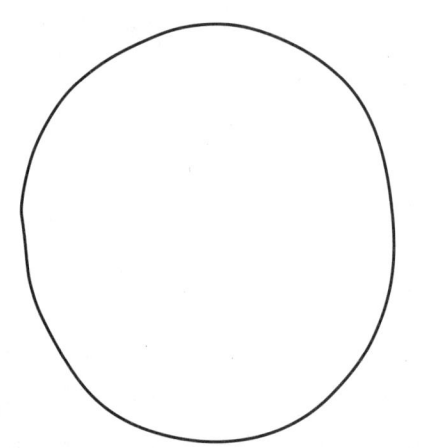

You don't speak Chinese, but you know that Ali's expression means fear. When you see her face, your brain communicates to you, telling you to _____

_____ behind you. Now you see the tiger, and your fear starts in your brain and tells you to _____.

Everyone runs out of the room to safety!

(See Appendix D for answers.)

Answer these questions to test your understanding of the reason we have feelings. Good luck!

1. Ali saw the tiger before you did, and you saw the fear on Ali's face. What was her fear telling you?

_____

_____

_____

2. What was your fear telling you to notice or pay attention to?

_____

_____

_____

3. You and Ali do not speak the same language, but you both had the same feeling. What was that feeling motivating you and Ali to do?

_____

_____

_____

(See Appendix D for answers.)

Types of Thoughts

FOR YOU TO KNOW

The brain and your mind are two different things. Your mind produces your imagination, attitude, thoughts, and feelings. Your brain is like a house for your mind.

Thoughts are things we tell ourselves. Our mind produces different types of thoughts. There are three types of thoughts that everyone has: feeling-mind thoughts, fact-mind thoughts, and full-mind thoughts.

Feeling-mind thoughts focus only on the feelings you have about a situation or an event. Feeling-mind thoughts make every situation feel big, intense, and like the end of the world. Feeling-mind thoughts can be very tricky, and we often get stuck in them.

Fact-mind thoughts are focused only on things you can observe—the facts of the situation. Your fact mind does not consider any of the feelings or wants of people in the situation. Using your fact mind does not change the intensity of your feelings like your feeling mind does. Your fact mind actually doesn't think about feelings at all.

When you mix together your feelings and the facts of the situation, you are using your full mind. Using your full mind is actually very hard because you have to experience uncomfortable feelings and make good choices at the same time.

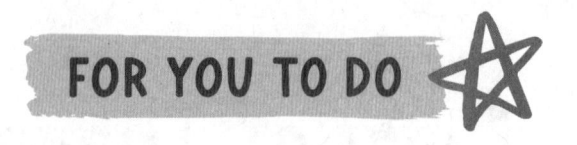

The diagram below illustrates the three types of thoughts you have. For each situation, shade in the diagram to show where the thoughts are coming from.

You get home from school, and your dad says you have to do your homework before you can watch any YouTube videos.

"I never get to have fun!"

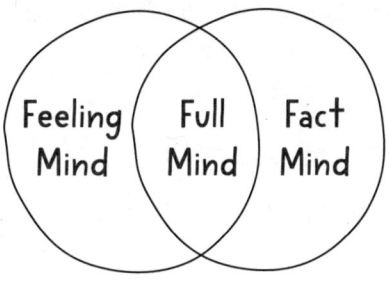

"I don't like doing my homework, and I can watch videos after I get it done."

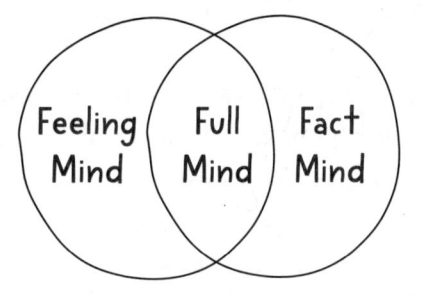

"I have to do my homework to pass in school."

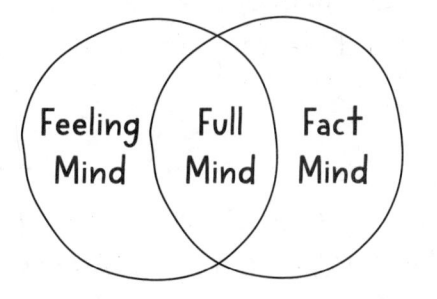

You're playing a board game with your neighbor Cole. You went first in the first round, and now Cole wants to go first.

"I really want to go first again. The right thing to do is give Cole a turn, even though I don't want to."

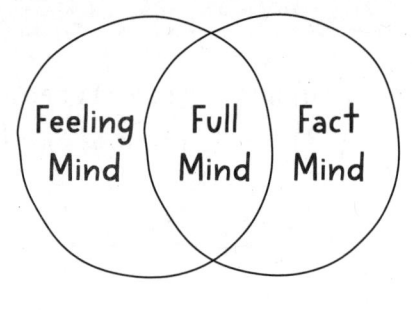

"Cole always gets to go first!"

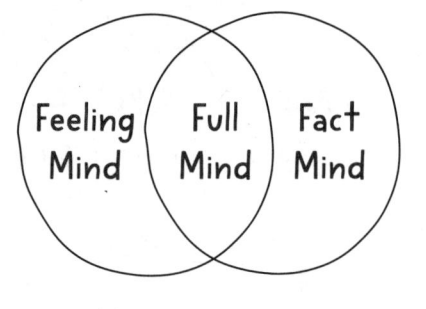

"Only one person can go first at time."

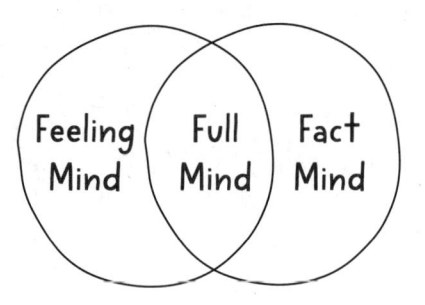

There are a lot more rules in third grade than second grade. You seem to be having more bad days recently.

"It's hard following rules at school, but I like to see my friends each day."

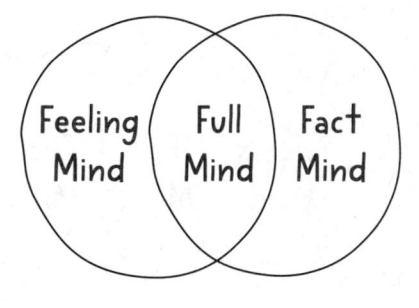

"I hate everything about school!"

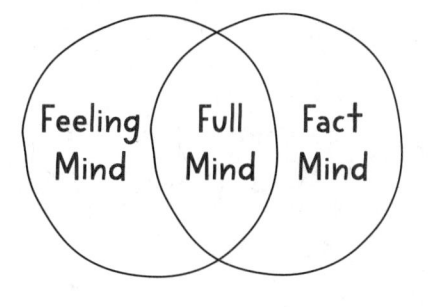

"Adults and teachers are in charge at school."

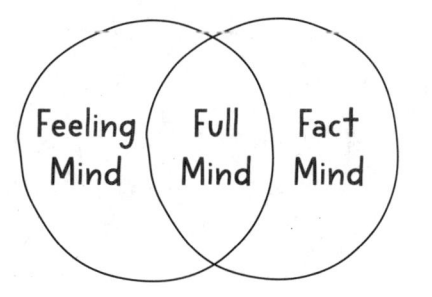

Your sister takes your iPad without asking and you're angry. You have the immediate urge to punch her.

"I hate her!"

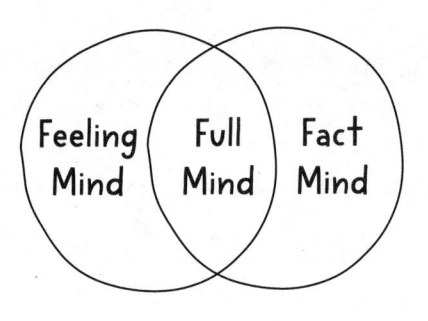

"There is only one iPad in the house."

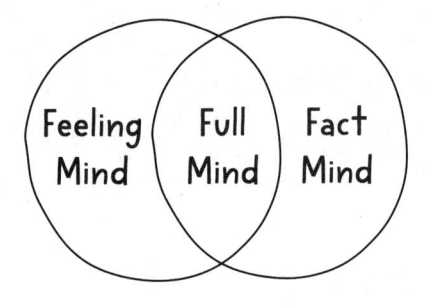

"I love my sister, and she makes me so mad sometimes!"

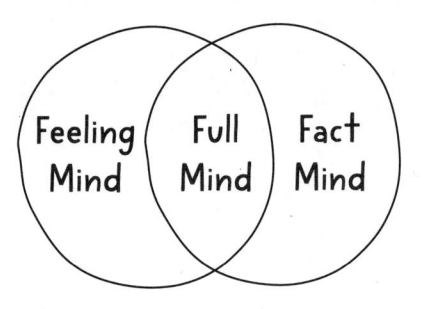

ACTIVITY 6

Your Thoughts

FOR YOU TO KNOW

You can have up to a thousand or more thoughts a day. With practice, people are able to change their thoughts even if they can't totally control them.

You have learned about the three types of thoughts you have. Depending on what is happening at the time, you might have thoughts from any one of the three categories. Without looking back, see if you can remember the three types of thinking. Good luck!

1. _____

2. _____

3. _____

Everyone has times when they get stuck in their feeling-mind thoughts. Use the lines below to write about a situation that you often seem to get stuck in. If you are unsure of a situation to use, ask an adult who knows you well.

_____

_____

_____

_____

_____

_____

_____

_____

_____

_____

_____

MORE ➔

_____

_____

_____

_____

_____

_____

_____

_____

Now draw a picture in the box to illustrate the situation.

Focusing on Understanding Anger

Anger is a strong feeling that can get real big very fast! In this section, we will learn more about the things that make us angry, how anger comes in different sizes, and how our thoughts can make it worse and actually keep us angry. Anger has a way of taking over our brain and our actions. This does not always lead to making the best decisions. Use the activities in this section to think about how anger sometimes takes control of your brain. With practice, you can learn to take back control and not let anger get you in trouble.

ACTIVITY 7

What Causes Anger?

FOR YOU TO KNOW

When you are blocked from reaching your goal or you don't get something you want, it is natural to feel angry.

Getting angry is a natural part of being alive. All people get angry at some point—for example, moms, dads, teachers, friends, and even professional athletes. There are certain situations where getting angry is totally normal. Sometimes people will say, "Just don't be angry," but it's never that easy.

FOR YOU TO DO

Listed on the next page are some things that cause anger for most people. Use the blank lines to write down an example of a time each situation has happened to you. Use the last three bullets to add any other specific situations that make you angry.

- You don't get what you want or need.

_____

_____

- Someone takes your things without asking.

_____

_____

- You think someone or something is unfair.

_____

_____

- Things don't go as you planned.

_____

_____

- Someone says something mean or disrespectful about you or someone you care about.

_____

_____

- You are not understanding something.

_____

_____

- _____

- _____

- _____

Anger Comes in Many Sizes

FOR YOU TO KNOW

Like most things in the world, feelings come in different sizes — small, medium, large, and sometimes even extra-large.

Like all feelings, anger comes in different sizes. What makes you only a little angry might make someone else very angry. It's important to recognize all the different words used to describe the different sizes of anger. Big anger is usually easier to identify because it is so uncomfortable.

On the next page are some of the words we use to describe the different experiences of anger. Even though each of these feels a little different, they are all a version of the same thing: anger.

ANGRY	AGGRAVATED	AGITATED	ANNOYED
BITTER	EXASPERATED	FIERCE	FRUSTRATED
FURIOUS	GROUCHY	GRUMPY	HOSTILE
INDIGNANT	IRRITABLE	IRRITATED	MAD
OUTRAGED	RAGING	VENGEFUL	WRATHFUL

FOR YOU TO DO

Can you add any words to the list in the box? Write them here.

_____   _____

_____   _____

Complete the word search on the next page to review and become familiar with the anger words listed on the previous page.

MORE

A	I	N	D	I	G	N	A	N	T	I	U	I	D
U	U	D	E	G	A	R	T	U	O	E	T	G	F
T	A	N	V	A	U	V	S	D	R	X	F	I	I
L	T	D	T	T	D	E	A	I	Y	A	R	R	E
U	G	R	A	G	I	N	G	R	H	S	U	R	R
F	G	S	R	E	A	G	I	R	C	P	S	I	C
H	O	S	T	I	L	E	T	I	U	E	T	T	E
T	Y	R	P	G	P	F	A	T	O	R	R	A	I
A	E	O	I	E	E	U	T	A	R	A	A	T	N
R	Y	R	G	N	A	L	E	B	G	T	T	E	G
W	B	I	T	T	E	R	D	L	A	E	E	D	M
G	R	U	M	P	Y	N	R	E	R	D	D	I	A
H	D	E	T	A	V	A	R	G	G	A	B	T	D
A	N	N	O	Y	E	D	S	U	O	I	R	U	F

FRUSTRATED   AGGRAVATED   FIERCE

VENGEFUL   HOSTILE   OUTRAGED

INDIGNANT   IRRATATED   WRATHFUL

IRRITABLE   EXASPERATED   AGITATED

BITTER   MAD   ANGRY

RAGING   ANNOYED   GRUMPY

FURIOUS   GROUCHY

(See Appendix D for answers.)

ACTIVITY 9

Your Anger Triggers

FOR YOU TO KNOW

An anger trigger is like the fuse on a firecracker. Once you light it, it burns quickly until the firecracker explodes.

Anger can feel different for each person. One of the goals of this workbook is for you to become more familiar with your own feelings of anger. Understanding what leads to your anger is important for learning how to catch anger before it gets out of control.

FOR YOU TO DO

Use these lines to write down the ten most common situations that lead to *you* being angry, in any order. You might not be able to think of ten at one time. That's okay; you can always come back to it.

1. _____

2. _____

3. _____

4. _____

5. _____

6. _____

7. _____

8. _____

9. _____

10. _____

Look at the list you just created, and put it into the chart that follows. Use 10 for the situation that leads to the most intense anger, and 1 for the least intense. Then, in the column on the right, write the word you would use to describe the exact feeling. A few examples have been included. Try to list at least one event and an anger word for each level of intensity.

If you need help, you can look back at the list of anger words in Activity 8. You might repeat some anger words, and that's okay. Remember, the goal is to become more familiar with your own feelings of anger.

RANK	EVENT	ANGER WORD
10.	EXAMPLE: My brother deleted my saved game!	Raging
9.		
8.		
7.		
6.		
5.		
4.	EXAMPLE: I can't figure out a math problem.	Frustrated
3.		
2.		
1.		

Catch It!

FOR YOU TO KNOW

People have a lot of different thoughts each day. Paying attention to, or catching, your thoughts is part of mindfulness, and doing it will take practice.

You know the different types of thoughts people have: feeling-mind thoughts, fact-mind thoughts, and full-mind thoughts. As you focus on anger, it will be important for you to notice the thoughts you have when you are feeling really big or growing anger. Many of the thoughts we have increase our anger and keep us angry. For example, sitting and thinking over and over again about an event that made you angry will actually make your anger bigger, because your thoughts are feeding your anger, helping it grow. You can learn to catch your feeling thoughts, check them, and then change them.

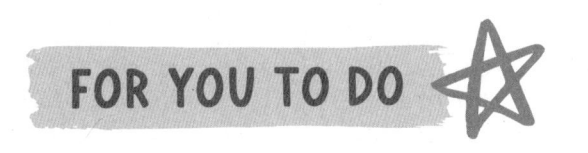

FOR YOU TO DO

This activity will help you learn to catch words that are warning signs for big anger thoughts. Read the words on the next page, and circle the ones that could feed anger or make it stronger; these are from your feeling mind. Underline the ones that are more balanced, not so dramatic; these could come from your full mind. Revisit Activity 5 if you need to. If you are not sure of the meaning of all the words, ask an adult for help.

help	sympathy	constantly
never	no way	respect
hate	compromise	unending
truce	forget it	revenge
kindness	absolutely not	negotiate
always	every time	refuse
deal	middle path	calm
forever	trust	patient

(See Appendix D for answers.)

ACTIVITY 11

Check It!

FOR YOU TO KNOW

Thoughts are so powerful that you can just think of something that might make you mad and you will start to feel angry—even if what you thought of isn't actually happening in that moment.

Thoughts and feelings both come from your mind. An event happens, and what you think about it leads to the feelings you have. Different thoughts can actually make your feelings grow bigger and more intense. Humans eat food to grow big. Your thoughts are like food for your feelings. The more you think about the thing that made you angry, the bigger your anger gets.

FOR YOU TO DO

Read Jake's story and underline the thoughts that are feeding his anger. Circle the thoughts that help his anger shrink.

Jake and his buddies like to play baseball during recess at school, and their team almost always wins. On Tuesday, Jake's team lost, and he was mad! The class lined up and headed inside for math. As the class was walking in, he could hear the guys from the winning team talking about how excited they were that they won. Jake thought, *I can't believe we lost. We should have won! The other team should not have won! They suck!*

Jake was clenching his fists as he walked into the classroom to find his seat. As he got his iPad out for math, one of his buddies walked by and said, "We did the best we could. We'll beat 'em next time." As Jake thought about this, he noticed that the knot in his stomach relaxed a bit, and he took a deep breath.

The teacher started math class by asking the students to go to exercise 20. Jake opened exercise 20, only to see that it was a word problem about a baseball team. He immediately thought, *I hate that we lost. We should have won.* Jake noticed that he was breathing heavily again and having a hard time listening to the directions for math. His anger was back!

Jake took one big deep breath and said to himself, *We'll play again tomorrow,* and he refocused on his schoolwork.

In this story there are at least five thoughts that feed the anger and make it bigger. Write these thoughts on the tentacles of the anger monster on the next page. Remember, these might be thoughts that come from your feelings or from thinking about the situation over and over again.

(See Appendix D for answers.)

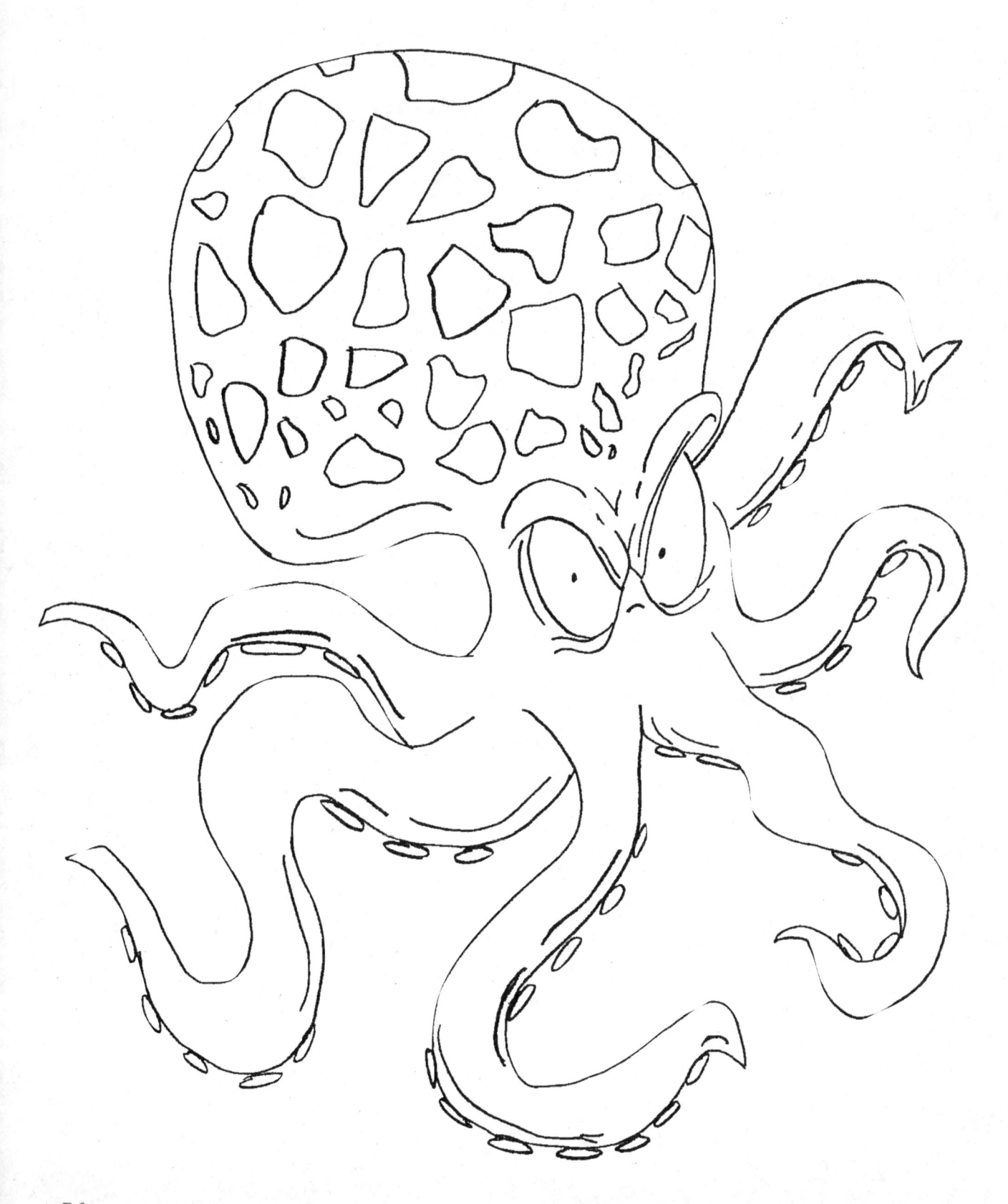

ACTIVITY
12

Change It!

FOR YOU TO KNOW

Changing your thoughts can change your feelings. Thinking about what first made you angry actually feeds your anger, making it bigger and bigger. Changing how you think about a situation can change the size of your anger.

You can change how you feel by changing what you're thinking about. If you watch a really sad movie, it might make you cry. That's because it makes you think about sad things happening. Anger works the same way. If you continue to think about what made you angry, you will stay angry. If you focus your mind on different thoughts, your feelings will change.

For example, imagine you wanted to spend all Saturday outside and woke up to find out it was going to rain all day. You would be pretty mad, but do you understand why? The why is very important.

Your goal was to be outside all day. It rained, which stopped you from being outside. It makes sense that you would be angry because now you can't do the fun things you had planned on. If you sit all day and think only about all the fun you're not having, your anger will grow bigger and bigger.

Remember, if you change your thoughts, you can change your feelings. Instead of thinking about how it's raining and wishing you could be outside, you can use your brain to think about fun things to do inside, which will make your anger get smaller and smaller as the day goes on.

There are **4** things you can do to change your thoughts during an angry moment:

1.

CHANGE WHAT YOU'RE SAYING TO YOURSELF.

For example, instead of saying to yourself, I should be outside having fun, say to yourself, I can't control the weather. I'll find something fun to do inside.

2.

CHANGE WHAT YOU'RE LOOKING AT.

For example, instead of sitting and staring out the window at the rain, put on your favorite movie and focus on that.

CHANGE WHAT YOU ARE DOING.

For example, instead of walking around the house complaining about not being outside, find something to do that will require your attention. That could be a video game, a puzzle, a craft project, or building something new with Legos.

4.

CHANGE WHERE YOU ARE.

For example, if sitting at home is hard because you keep thinking about the rain, ask your parent if you can go to the library or the store.

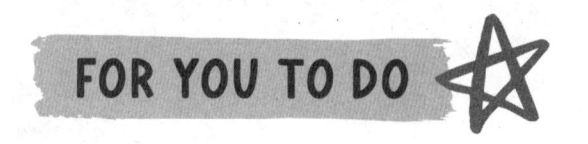

Read the following situations, and write about how you would try to change your thoughts to change your anger.

Your brother went into your Minecraft world and destroyed the bridges you just built. You're sitting at dinner with your family, and your brother is sitting across from you. You keep thinking to yourself, *I can't believe he destroyed my bridges! He's such a jerk!* Change what you're saying to yourself to change your anger. What could you think instead?

_____

_____

_____

_____

You've been wanting to use your allowance for a new skateboard, but your parents have said no. A new skateboard is all you can think of, and you are looking online at your favorites. The more you look at them, the more angry you get because you can't have one. Change what you're looking at to change your anger. What could you look at instead?

_____

_____

_____

_____

You are playing basketball with the kids in the neighborhood, and one kid keeps calling you names. You notice that you are getting more and more angry, and your anger is getting harder to control. Change what you're doing to change your anger. What could you do instead?

_____

_____

_____

_____

_____

_____

You're sitting in the family room playing with your Switch, and your brother comes in and keeps interrupting you with questions. He is annoying you, and he just won't stop. Change where you are to change your anger. Where could you go instead?

_____

_____

_____

_____

_____

_____

ACTIVITY 13

Anger in Your Body

FOR YOU TO KNOW

Your brain sends signals to your entire body one to two times every second. All together, this adds up to between 86 thousand and 172 thousand signals coming from your brain to your body every day.

When you are angry, your brain releases chemicals that affect not only your brain but also how your body and muscles feel. Big anger will feel big in your body. Anger will be easier to control if you can learn to identify it when it is small. Paying attention to how your body feels when you are angry will help you do this. Complete the activity on the next page, and remember that you may have to go back to it time and time again to add to it. When you are first getting familiar with how anger feels in your body, it takes a lot of patience and practice.

FOR YOU TO DO

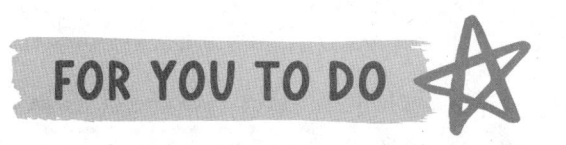

Color or add to this picture to show where you feel anger in your body.

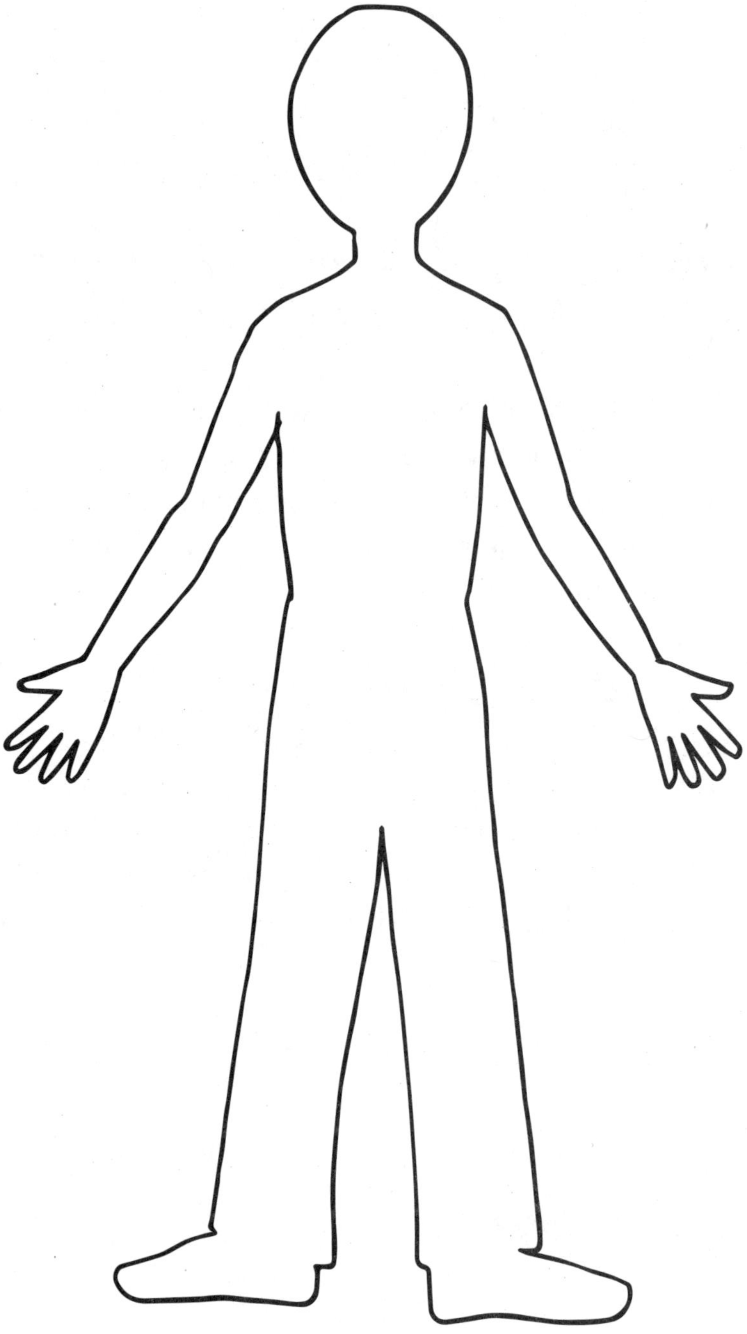

Expressions of Anger

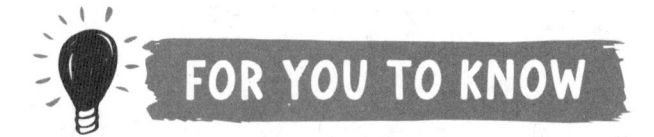

FOR YOU TO KNOW

Anger is just one of over twenty-five different feelings that human beings naturally experience in life.

It's tempting to think that you'll never get angry again so anger will never be a problem, but this is impossible. Everybody feels anger, and you are always going to have situations that make you angry. When you get angry and then get in trouble, it's not the anger that gets you in trouble—it's your actions.

FOR YOU TO DO

You've already worked on noticing how anger feels in your body. Now, take some time to think about what you do when you're angry. Fill in the questions below about each size of anger, with 10 being the strongest anger you have felt.

Here's an example:

How does it feel in my body: <u>rock in my stomach</u>

What I am doing (behaviors): <u>scrunched face, heavy sigh</u>

You may also find it helpful to ask an adult who knows you well what they notice you do as you get angry.

ANGER INTENSITY ⚡

10

How it feels in my body: _____

What I am doing (behaviors): _____

8-9

How it feels in my body: _____

What I am doing (behaviors): _____

6-7

How it feels in my body: _____

What I am doing (behaviors): _____

5

How it feels in my body: _____

What I am doing (behaviors): _____

3-4

How it feels in my body: _____

What I am doing (behaviors): _____

1-2

How it feels in my body: _____

What I am doing (behaviors): _____

ACTIVITY 15

Anger Urges

Before you take any action, you have a thought, even though it may happen so fast you don't notice it. We call these thoughts "urges." When you think about something you want to do—really, really want to do—that is an urge.

When anger is high, it takes over your brain and urges you to act a certain way. The trick is that you don't have to listen to every urge you have. You can actually do nothing and wait for it to pass, or you can do the opposite. It's like playing a game of Simon Says. When the leader says, "Stomp your left foot," you can almost feel your foot move, but you don't do it because they didn't say "Simon Says." Take a few minutes to play Simon Says, and see if you notice any urges you have. Practicing this will help you learn to notice urges you have when you're angry.

FOR YOU TO DO

The chart below shows the steps that lead up to acting on anger.
Fill in the missing information.

SITUATION	THOUGHT	URGE	ACTION
YOUR DAD MAKES YOU GET OFF THE VIDEO GAME.	No! I haven't finished my game.	I want to break something!	Throw the controller against the wall.
THE TEACHER DOES NOT CALL ON YOU FIRST IN CLASS, EVEN THOUGH YOU HAVE YOUR HAND UP.	This is not fair!		
YOUR BROTHER SNEAKS INTO YOUR ROOM AND DESTROYS YOUR LEGO CREATION.	What a jerk!	I'm going to break his stuff.	
YOU FIND OUT THAT YOUR BEST FRIEND TOLD A LIE ABOUT YOU TO ANOTHER FRIEND.			Tell everyone in class a lie about your friend.

ACTIVITY 16

Slow It Down

FOR YOU TO KNOW

Anger messages move through your brain and the rest of your body faster than you can imagine. Your brain and the rest of your body send messages back and forth at speeds up to 268 miles per hour.

So far in this book, you've covered a lot. You've worked on identifying the different types of thoughts you have and situations that cause anger. You've learned how feeling-mind thoughts make your anger grow stronger. We've also talked about identifying how anger feels in your body.

The fastest animal on Earth is the cheetah, who can run seventy miles an hour. Turtles walk only three to four miles per hour. That is pretty slow! When you practice controlling your anger, it's better to think like a turtle than a cheetah.

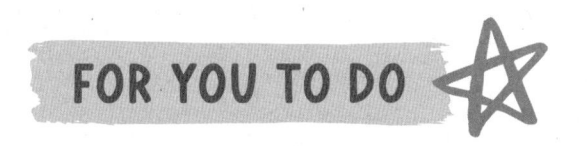

FOR YOU TO DO

Use the following worksheet to slow yourself down and record the different parts of a recent anger situation. This worksheet is also available online at http://www.newharbinger.com/47278. You can print several copies to practice on; if you need help, ask an adult. The more you practice, the easier it will become.

Situation that causes anger:

What my body feels like:

Urges (what I want to do):

Actions (what I actually did):

Feeling-Mind Thoughts:

Anger Messages

FOR YOU TO KNOW

In the days of cavemen, our feelings would send messages to our brain that would actually save our lives by warning us of danger. Even today, our feelings are our brain's way of communicating to us and others.

Each of the feelings listed below is sending a different **message**.

FEELING	MESSAGE
ANXIETY/FEAR	DANGER! RUN! PROTECT YOURSELF!
DISGUST	GROSS! DON'T TOUCH IT!
GUILT	YOU MADE A MISTAKE. ASK FOR FORGIVENESS. APOLOGIZE.
PRIDE	YOU DID WELL! TELL OTHERS ABOUT YOUR SUCCESS.
LOVE	SPEND MORE TIME WITH THE PERSON.

Anger can send us helpful and unhelpful messages. Read the messages below and circle or color the messages that are helpful.

This goal is important to me. I need to problem solve.

I don't like what's happening. I need to get an adult's help.

This person is being mean. I need to let them know I don't like what is happening.

I lost the game! I need to practice more. I can get better and win next time.

I'm right! I don't care what they say!

She cheated! I'm gonna destroy her project.

He took my spot. I'm gonna get him!

(See Appendix D for answers.)

Wait It Out!
After the Anger Passes

FOR YOU TO KNOW

Feelings are like rainstorms: they don't last forever. If you wait long enough, the rain will stop and you can go back outside. If you wait long enough, anger also passes.

When you get angry, it's important to remember that the feeling doesn't last forever. The feeling of anger, just like all your other feelings, goes away after a while. What you might notice is that once the anger passes, you have some aftereffects. You have to give your brain some extra time to return to normal. It's like leaving a water park. You're not in the water anymore, but you are still wet. You need to wait a little while to dry off before getting in the car.

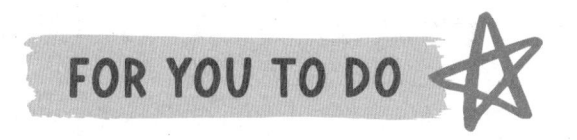

FOR YOU TO DO

The list on the next page includes some common things that happen after a person has been angry. Read through them, and use the blank lines to add any others you have noticed in yourself. Color in the circles next to the three that happen to you the most.

O Thinking **only** about the situation that made you angry and nothing else

O Thinking **over and over** about the situation that made you angry

O Talking to others **over and over** about the situation that made you angry

O Thinking about the person who made you angry

O Remembering other times that the same thing has happened

O Imagining situations in the future where you might be angry

O Imagining what you will do or say the next time the situation happens

O Feeling shaky

O Breathing heavily

O _____

_____

O _____

_____

O _____

_____

Several positive things could come out of waiting for your anger to pass. This chart shows some positive things (pros) and negative things (cons) of waiting for your anger to pass versus acting on it in the moment. Some of the chart has been filled in. Take some time to fill in more of the pros and cons.

	WHAT POSITIVE THINGS COULD HAPPEN?	WHAT NEGATIVE THINGS COULD HAPPEN?
WAIT IT OUT	Make better choices Not hurt others	Feel uncomfortable Not easy

	WHAT POSITIVE THINGS COULD HAPPEN?	WHAT NEGATIVE THINGS COULD HAPPEN?
ACT ON IT	Feel good for a quick moment	My behaviors hurt others My friendships get damaged

ACTIVITY
19

Dear Anger

FOR YOU TO KNOW

Struggling with anger does not mean you are a bad person.
Anger is only one part of who you are.

When you have intense anger, it can feel like the anger is bossing you around and you have no choice but to physically act out. When this happens a lot, you may start to think you are a bad person. The truth is, with practice you can always be in control of your thoughts and actions. Instead of your anger being the one to give the orders, you get to be in control of what you do.

FOR YOU TO DO

Place an empty chair across from you and imagine that your anger is sitting in that chair. This is the same anger that takes control of your thoughts and tries to take control of your behaviors! Write a letter to your anger to let it know how you feel and what you plan to do in the future when you are angry.

Dear Anger

Anger Can Hurt Others

When we get angry, we often lash out at other people. This is because making and keeping friends can be hard, and interacting with others can be challenging. We've reviewed the basic feelings, learned about three different ways of thinking, and focused on understanding your anger.

In this section, we are going to look a little closer at how your anger might be affecting your friendships and making it hard to get along with other people.

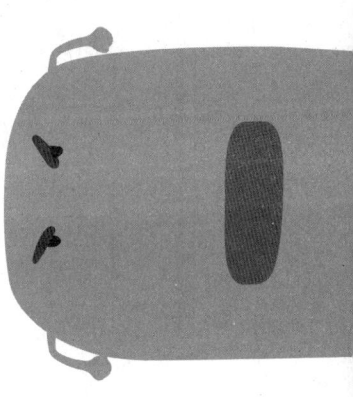

When Anger Ruins Friendships

FOR YOU TO KNOW

All friends have disagreements with each other from time to time—this is totally normal. But friendships are important, and good friends treat each other with respect, even when they are angry.

Have you ever been to the beach and built a sandcastle? Sandcastles can be tricky. It takes time to build one, and you might make mistakes along the way, having to stop and fix things until it looks like you want and is strong enough to stand. Once you have your sandcastle built, you have to watch out for the waves coming in from the ocean. If the waves hit the sandcastle, it will slowly crumble.

Your friendships are like sandcastles, and the ocean waves are like the actions of your anger. If your angry actions keep hitting your friendships, they can crumble over time. And when anger becomes so intense that it controls your behaviors, it can start to slowly destroy your friendships.

There are ways to keep the waves from hitting your sandcastle. You can build a deep moat, or trench, around your castle. This will protect your sandcastle no matter how big the waves get. Like the moat around your sandcastle, the coping skills you learn in this book will help protect your friendships from the waves of anger.

FOR YOU TO DO

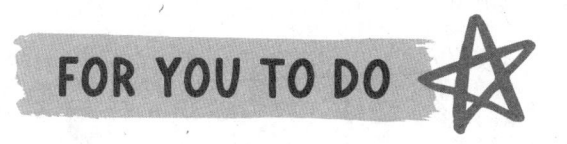

Color the picture, and label the waves with anger actions that slowly destroy friendships.

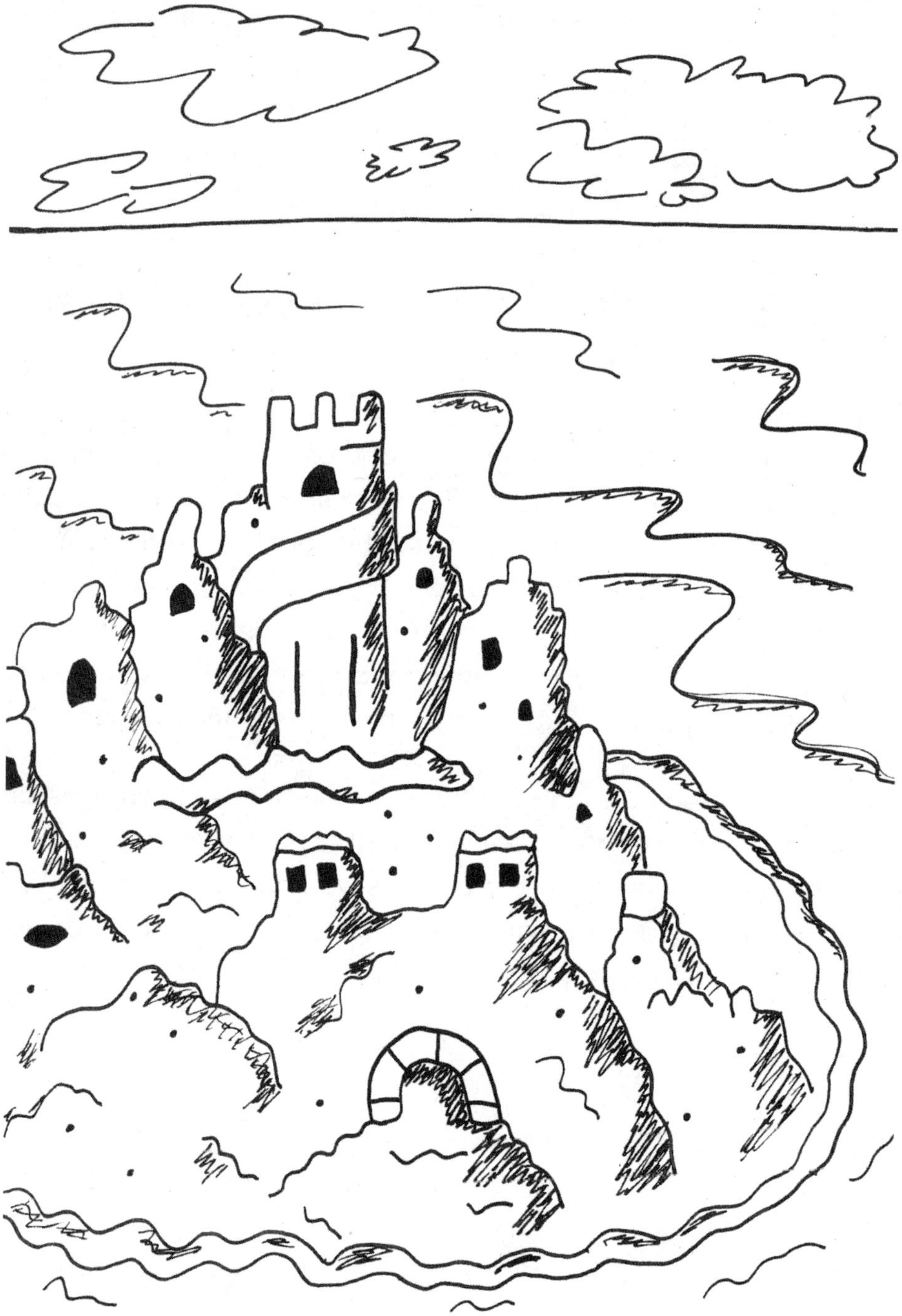

What Messages Are You Sending?

FOR YOU TO KNOW

Friendships are built with actions you show people over and over, not with words.

There are reasons we have feelings. One of those reasons is to send messages to ourselves and also to people around us. Every time we are around other people, we are sending them messages with our words and actions. The feelings you have will change the messages you send. For example, when you are feeling happy, you may be smiling and friendly with other people. This sends the message to other people that you are in a good mood and want to be around them. It may tell other people that you are a nice person to be around.

In this activity, we are going to think about what messages our anger is sending to other people. This is important to think about, because sometimes our anger gets so big and intense that it sends messages we don't want to send. When this happens over and over again, others start to see us as an angry person or a person who is not fun to be around.

FOR YOU TO DO

For each question, put a check mark next to the answer that is closest to what you are most likely to do. Then keep reading to see what your answers might say about you.

When someone makes you feel angry, what are you most likely to do?

1. Scream, push, or hit them.

2. Let out a big sigh.

3. Walk away and take a break.

While at recess, you lose the kickball game. What are you most likely to do?

1. Stomp off and refuse to play anymore.

2. Shake hands with the winning team.

3. Feel disappointed and move on to try a new game.

You and your friend are playing a game of Monopoly, and you lose. What are you most likely to do?

1. Scream, "No! You cheated!" and knock the pieces off the table.

2. Set up the board to play again.

3. Let out a big sigh and have a sad face.

You're playing a video game, and your dad comes in to say you have to go to bed. You want to keep playing. What are you most likely to do?

1. Yell, "No! Get out of here!" and refuse to end the game.

2. Say, "Uggg—okay," save your game, and put the console away.

3. Smile and happily put the game away.

You have been working on a new Lego creation for over a week. Your brother knocks it off the table, and it breaks. What are you most likely to do?

1. Shove your brother to the ground and call him a loser.

2. Yell out, "No! Look what you did!"

3. Scream, "Stop! You destroyed it!"

Look over your answers. How many 1s did you get? The 1s are all actions and words that show you are letting anger control you and damage your relationships. Mostly 1s means you need to continue to practice being angry without acting on your anger.

ACTIVITY 22

What Kind of Person Do You Want to Be?

"Try your best to make goodness attractive. That's one of the toughest assignments you'll ever be given."
—Mr. Rogers

Think of the kids in your class. There are kids who you know will help you if you need it. There are kids who don't play fair or always have to go first. There are kids who you can be sure will share, and then there are kids who never seem to share.

When you have a hard time with anger, it can begin to change the kind of person you are, and other people may begin to notice. While you are learning to manage your anger, take some time to think about how you interact with others and what you want other people to think about you.

Think of some of the people you spend time with. What makes these people good friends? What makes some people hard to spend time with? Why do you like to hang out with some people and not others?

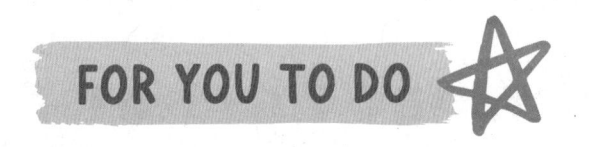

Values are traits or things that you think are important and represent the type of person you want to be. Below is a list of fifteen common values and actions that go along with each one. In the column on the left, place a check mark next to ten values you think are important and represent the type of person you want to be. If you need help with this activity, ask a trusted adult.

✓	VALUE	ACTION
	HONESTY	TELLING THE TRUTH
	KINDNESS	USING KIND WORDS
	HELPING OTHERS	HOLDING THE DOOR OPEN FOR SOMEONE BEHIND YOU
	SAFETY	NOT PHYSICALLY HURTING OTHERS
	RESPONSIBILITY	TAKING GOOD CARE OF YOUR THINGS
	FRIENDSHIP	TREATING PEERS NICELY IN ORDER TO KEEP FRIENDSHIPS
	GRATITUDE	BEING THANKFUL FOR THE THINGS YOU HAVE IN YOUR LIFE
	LEARNING	WORKING HARD IN SCHOOL TO LEARN A NEW SUBJECT
	TEAMWORK	WORKING TOGETHER WITH OTHERS TO ACHIEVE A GOAL
	BRAVERY/COURAGE	TRYING THINGS EVEN WHEN YOU ARE NERVOUS OR SCARED
	SHARING/GENEROSITY	ALLOWING OTHERS A CHANCE TO USE SHARED ITEMS
	POLITENESS	USING GOOD MANNERS WHEN INTERACTING WITH OTHER PEOPLE
	EFFORT	TRYING YOUR BEST AT THE THINGS YOU DO
	LISTENING	LISTENING TO FRIENDS WHEN THEY NEED SOMEONE TO TALK TO
	TRUSTWORTHINESS	DOING WHAT YOU SAY YOU WILL DO

MORE FOR YOU TO DO

Now that you have thought about the kind of person you want to be, let's think about what actions can help you do this. Write each value you chose, and add an idea of what you could do to make this true in your life—in other words, an action that goes with the value. One has been done for you.

Value (what's important to me): <u>Kindness</u>

Action (what I can do to show my value): <u>Help a kid who drops their things in the hallway</u>

Value: _____

Action: _____

_____

Value: _____

Action: _____

_____

Value: _____

Action: _____

_____

Value: _____

Action: _____

_____

Value: _____

Action: _____

_____

Value: _____

Action: _____

_____

Value: _____

Action: _____

_____

Value: _____

Action: _____

_____

Value: _____

Action: _____

_____

Value: _____

Action: _____

_____

ACTIVITY 23

Repairing Relationships Affected by Anger

FOR YOU TO KNOW

When anger flares up, it gets in the way of relationships. It is normal for people to have disagreements every once in a while. When you do have disagreements with friends (or family members), it is important to take steps to repair any damage.

The word "apologize" comes from a Greek word meaning "give an account" or "explain." To fix a relationship, you can apologize and promise to change your behavior. While you are still practicing managing your anger, you might need to do this more often. It takes practice to change your behavior, and everyone makes mistakes along the way.

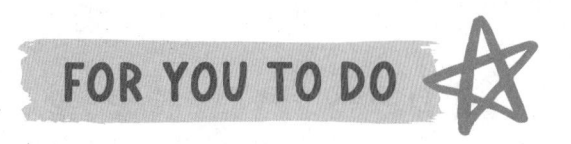

Read each situation and then write down what the person could say and do to apologize.

You are playing video games with your friend, and you lose on level 4. You are so angry that you throw your controller at your friend and call them a cheater.

WORDS TO APOLOGIZE:	ACTIONS TO APOLOGIZE:

You are learning a new chapter in math and are finding it very confusing. You do not understand what the teacher is explaining. This makes you angry at yourself, and you feel a little embarrassed in front of your classmates. Jason, sitting next to you, raises his hand and gets the answer correct. You throw a pencil at him, saying, "Nerd!" and end up having to go to the principal's office.

WORDS TO APOLOGIZE:	ACTIONS TO APOLOGIZE:

You're lining up at recess to head back inside. You are racing to be at the front of the line, and your classmate Shawn beats you there. He got to be first yesterday, and you are so angry that without even thinking, you push him to the ground.

WORDS TO APOLOGIZE:	ACTIONS TO APOLOGIZE:

You had a rough day at school, and now your mom wants you to go to the store with her. All you really want to do is veg out and play video games. Your mom insists that you go with her. You get mad, call her names, and say, "I hate that you're my mom!"

WORDS TO APOLOGIZE:	ACTIONS TO APOLOGIZE:

ACTIVITY 24

Make a Deal

FOR YOU TO KNOW

Having a disagreement with friends can be helpful:
you can grow closer and learn how to be better friends.

All people have disagreements: they are a normal part of life. What's important when you have a disagreement with someone is how you react or how you treat the other person. Making a deal is a way of getting past an obstacle with someone. Some people call this "meeting in the middle" or "negotiating." Making a deal means that when each person wants something different, or thinks something different, they are willing to give a little to the other person until they can reach a compromise. To practice this, you have to be able to remain calm and think about how the other person is feeling in the situation. This can be hard to do when you are angry.

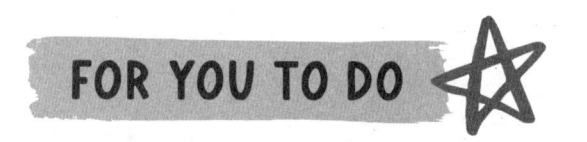

FOR YOU TO DO

Read these situations, and circle the choice you think is the best option for making a deal, or reaching a compromise. There may be more than one answer.

72

1. Josh and Christina both want pizza for dinner. Mom is letting them decide where they want to go. Josh wants Papa John's and Christina wants Little Caesars.

   a. Go to Papa John's.

   b. Go to Papa John's this week and Little Caesars next week.

   c. Go to Little Caesars.

   d. Go home and make homemade pizza.

2. The Taylor family is going on a road trip to the beach for spring break. Joe and Chris both want to sit in the front seat and are fighting before they even leave the house! Their mom tells them to compromise and make a deal.

   a. Joe and Chris both ride in the backseat the entire trip.

   b. Joe and Chris agree to take turns in the front seat, changing at every stop.

   c. Joe gets to ride in the front on the way to the beach, and Chris gets to ride in the front on the way home.

   d. Joe and Chris refuse to compromise, and the family can't leave the house.

3. Audrey wants a new bike. The one she really wants is $100 more than her mom is willing to spend.

   a. Audrey's mom pays for the whole thing because that bike is what Audrey wants.

   b. Audrey's mom says the bike she already has is good enough.

   c. Audrey and her mom decide to split the cost of the new bike. Audrey uses her allowance to pay for her half.

   d. Audrey refuses to talk with her mom about brainstorming ideas. She wants the new bike now!

(See Appendix D for answers.)

Pushing Back Against Anger

Anger is a very strong feeling, but you don't have to let anger take control of your actions. You can push back against anger when you feel it growing inside you. In this section, we will go over coping skills you already have and then learn some new ones you can use to help control your anger and also keep your relationships safe and happy.

Remember that the goal is not to ever get angry. The goal is to be able to feel angry (like all people do) and still stay in control of your behaviors. That takes a lot of practice!

What Tools Have You Tried?

FOR YOU TO KNOW

Taking care of things, like your house or bike, requires tools. Taking care of your feelings and friendships also requires tools, but they are a different kind. We use these tools with our minds, thoughts, and actions to improve the way we manage our anger and help us take care of the people and things that are important to us.

So far in this book we've reviewed these seven ways to manage your thoughts, feelings, and actions. Review them and use the list to help you complete the For You to Do.

✔ **Full Mind** (Activity 5): Use your full mind to balance the facts of the situation with the feelings you are having to make a wise decision.

✔ **Catch It** (Activity 10): Stop and notice what is going on inside and outside of you. How are you feeling? Where do you feel it in your body? How big is your feeling?

✔ **Check It** (Activity 11): Check all the information you have. Are you looking at all sides of the story, or are you focusing only on your feeling thoughts?

✔ **Change It** (Activity 12): Change your thoughts on purpose. Focus your thinking on something else until your anger gets smaller.

✔ **Slow It Down** (Activity 16): Anger sneaks up on you very fast and can feel like it takes over. Slow down on purpose to stay in control.

✔ **Wait It Out** (Activity 18): Anger does not last forever. Wait for the anger to pass before acting.

✔ **Make a Deal** (Activity 24): Can you make a deal? Look for a way to help each person feel better about the outcome. You have to be willing to give up a little.

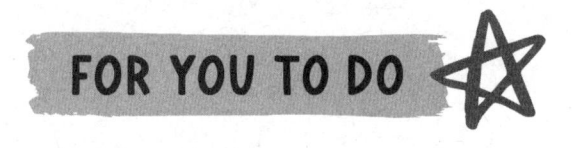

Think of the tools you have tried in the past to calm yourself down when you were angry. List them below, and then rate each on a scale of 1 to 5 to show how well it has worked for you.

Tool I have tried: _____

_____

1	**2**	**3**	**4**	**5**
I COULDN'T STAND IT FOR EVEN ONE MINUTE.		I WAS ABLE TO STAY SOMEWHAT CALM.		I WAS ABLE TO CONTROL ANGER AND RESIST URGES.

Tool I have tried: _____

_____

1	**2**	**3**	**4**	**5**
I COULDN'T STAND IT FOR EVEN ONE MINUTE.		I WAS ABLE TO STAY SOMEWHAT CALM.		I WAS ABLE TO CONTROL ANGER AND RESIST URGES.

Tool I have tried: _____

_____

1	**2**	**3**	**4**	**5**
I COULDN'T STAND IT FOR EVEN ONE MINUTE.		I WAS ABLE TO STAY SOMEWHAT CALM.		I WAS ABLE TO CONTROL ANGER AND RESIST URGES.

Tool I have tried: _____

_____

1	**2**	**3**	**4**	**5**
I COULDN'T STAND IT FOR EVEN ONE MINUTE.		I WAS ABLE TO STAY SOMEWHAT CALM.		I WAS ABLE TO CONTROL ANGER AND RESIST URGES.

Tool I have tried: _____

_____

1	**2**	**3**	**4**	**5**
I COULDN'T STAND IT FOR EVEN ONE MINUTE.		I WAS ABLE TO STAY SOMEWHAT CALM.		I WAS ABLE TO CONTROL ANGER AND RESIST URGES.

Tool I have tried: _____

_____

1	**2**	**3**	**4**	**5**
I COULDN'T STAND IT FOR EVEN ONE MINUTE.		I WAS ABLE TO STAY SOMEWHAT CALM.		I WAS ABLE TO CONTROL ANGER AND RESIST URGES.

SEEDS

FOR YOU TO KNOW

When we do the right things to take care of our mind and body, it is easier for us to also take care of our feelings.

Have you ever helped with a garden or cared for a plant? There are a lot of things to think about and pay attention to when you're in charge of a living thing. You have to think about the soil you use and the amount of sun and water the plant gets. Taking care of your feelings is also a big job, and there is a lot to think about. A good way to remember all these things is to think about SEEDS in your garden. Paying attention to your SEEDS will help you manage your feelings better.

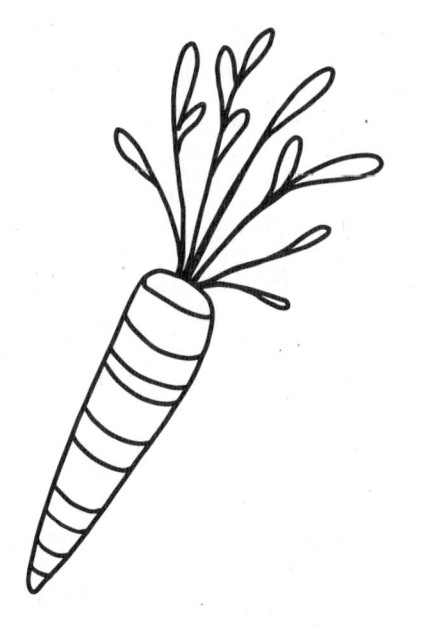

S—Sleep. Getting enough sleep each night is very important for your brain and helps you do your best during the day. Kids need between nine and eleven hours of sleep each night. How much sleep do you get? Do you notice that you have a better day after a good night's sleep?

E—Eating healthy foods. The food you eat is fuel for your brain and the rest of your body, which is important because they have to work together to handle your feelings. Do you eat enough fruits and vegetables? Are there some healthy foods you could focus on eating more of?

E—Exercise. It is important to get one hour or more of exercise each day. Even getting small amounts of exercise and movement each day helps your body work better. What kinds of things do you do for exercise? How often do you exercise? Is this something you can do more of?

D—Downtime. Take a break to be by yourself, read a book, or do something you enjoy, like a hobby. Even if you take just five minutes to relax, it can help you be prepared for the next event where you might have big feelings.

S—Socializing. While you most likely enjoy spending time with friends, it is important to keep a balance between socializing and being on your own. Think of the all the activities you have each week. Do you enjoy all of them? Do you ever feel like you need a break?

FOR YOU TO DO

Use this chart to write down the details of what you did to maintain your SEEDS for one week. At http://www.newharbinger.com/47278, you can download additional copies of this worksheet to use weekly while you are practicing the skills in this book.

	SUNDAY	MONDAY	TUESDAY	WEDNESDAY	THURSDAY	FRIDAY	SATURDAY
SLEEP							
EATING HEALTHY FOODS							
EXERCISE							
DOWNTIME							
SOCIALIZING							

Building Strength

FOR YOU TO KNOW

You build strength when you complete activities or tasks that are just a little challenging but make you feel good once you've finished. These things increase your sense of confidence and tend to be things you work on a little each day, in small steps.

When you are playing a video game, you usually have more than one life. For example, in Super Mario Brothers, you get three lives on each level. As you play, your character gets weaker with each mistake until you lose all three lives. There are things you can do in video games to build strength, and there are ways in real life that you can build strength. Building strength is important so that you are strong when big anger hits.

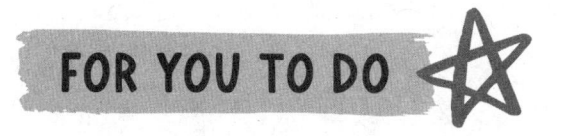

FOR YOU TO DO

Here are some examples of building strength:

- Learning a new trick on your bike after practicing for several days

- Working on organizing all your Legos, doing a little bit each day

- Learning to play guitar, doing a little each day

- Building your new Lego creation, one step at a time

- Practicing drawing dinosaurs, a little each day

On the lines below, list a few of the things you can do to build strength.

_____

_____

_____

_____

_____

_____

Refueling

FOR YOU TO KNOW

If a car runs out of gas, it will roll to a stop and won't even start. Your feelings are similar. Every once in a while, you have to refuel.

When you are feeling angry, that feeling can quickly take over your whole day. There can be times when you are so angry that you are able to notice only the bad things that are happening to you. It is important to learn to refuel, by paying attention to the positive things that are happening as well. You can also learn to engage in some positive activities on purpose when you are having a bad day.

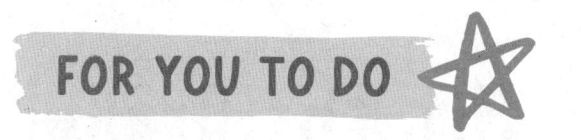

Doing activities you enjoy is a way of increasing positive thoughts and memories and decreasing negative or angry thoughts. Below are some ideas of things you can do when you're having a bad day to refuel yourself and build your strength. Use the blank lines to add things you like to do.

O Go for a walk	O Work on your Legos
O Play with your pet	O Text or direct message a friend
O Do a puzzle	O Make a TikTok video
O Play a video game	O Make a card for someone
O Ride your bike	O Play a board game or cards
O Read a book	O Listen to your favorite music
O Play catch	O _____
O Go outside	O _____
O Watch your favorite movie	O _____
O Sing along to your favorite song	O _____
O Dance to your favorite music	O _____

Hit the Brake!

FOR YOU TO KNOW

Paying attention to the feeling of anger in your body is a very important tool. If you can catch it sneaking up on you, you'll be able to hit the brake and slow it down when you need to.

Think of the last time you were riding your bike and needed to slow down or stop. What did you do? You probably hit the brake or maybe even used your feet as a brake to slow yourself down. You can learn to do this same thing when the feeling of anger begins to build up inside and take over. You can hit the BRAKE!

B — Take a deep **Breath**. Deep breathing tells your brain to slow down.

R — **Relax** your muscles; shake 'em out.

A — **Ask** your fact mind to help you see the facts of the situation. You can also **Ask** an adult for help.

K — Be **Kind**. Be kind to both yourself and others.

E — **Enter** the situation again when you are calm and ready.

Sometimes anger is so strong and quick that it can sneak up on you before you even notice. Using your BRAKE takes a lot of practice for both kids and adults.

FOR YOU TO DO

Ask an adult to help you make copies of the tokens below. You can also download the tokens at http://www.newharbinger.com/47278. Find two containers, one for blank tokens and one for completed tokens. When anyone in your family—including you—uses their BRAKE tool, give them a token and write down on the back what they did. Collect them in the container for completed tokens, and choose a goal as a family of something fun to do once it is full.

Adults can catch kids using BRAKE and kids can catch adults using BRAKE too. Everyone needs to practice!

⭐ BRAKE ⭐	⭐ BRAKE ⭐	⭐ BRAKE ⭐
GOOD JOB! YOU USED YOUR BRAKES TO MAKE A BETTER CHOICE! FROM: TO:	**GOOD JOB!** YOU USED YOUR BRAKES TO MAKE A BETTER CHOICE! FROM: TO:	**GOOD JOB!** YOU USED YOUR BRAKES TO MAKE A BETTER CHOICE! FROM: TO:
⭐ BRAKE ⭐	⭐ BRAKE ⭐	⭐ BRAKE ⭐
GOOD JOB! YOU USED YOUR BRAKES TO MAKE A BETTER CHOICE! FROM: TO:	**GOOD JOB!** YOU USED YOUR BRAKES TO MAKE A BETTER CHOICE! FROM: TO:	**GOOD JOB!** YOU USED YOUR BRAKES TO MAKE A BETTER CHOICE! FROM: TO:

Big Deal or Little Deal?

FOR YOU TO KNOW

Big feelings can become like a Snapchat filter and change the way you see the world around you.

When you are angry, your feeling mind can trick you into thinking that everything happening is the worst thing that has ever happened! Your feeling mind tells you that everything is a big deal when, if you were in full mind (a mixture of both feelings and facts), you would be able to see that not everything is a big deal and most things are actually little deals.

The Big Deal or Little Deal questions are:

- Am I safe?

- Am I treating others safely or the way I want to be treated?

- Can I ask an adult near me for help?

- Have I used my tools before acting?

- Can I put myself in the other person's shoes? What could they be thinking or feeling?

- Are my feelings too high, making it impossible for me to think clearly?

- Have I waited for my anger to pass before choosing my actions?

These questions are great tools to use with your BRAKE tool.

FOR YOU TO DO

Read this story and answer the questions that follow.

Jason is in fourth grade and in the same class as his twin sister, Brianna. Jason's favorite subjects are math and science. Jason has a hard time with reading and is slower at reading than his classmates, but he has never talked to anyone about this before. Brianna loves reading and is really good at it.

Their class has an assignment over the weekend: to finish three chapters in the book they are reading. Jason and Brianna are both sitting at the kitchen table, reading. Brianna finishes and begins to pack up her school supplies so she can go outside to play with friends. Jason notices that Brianna is done and immediately becomes frustrated with himself for taking longer to finish the assignment. He feels his muscles tightening up and his breathing change.

As Brianna moves past him to leave, he reaches out and knocks her book out of her hand. Brianna screams, "Hey, what did you do that for?" Jason replies, "There's no way you're done. You must have skipped the last chapter." Brianna says, "No I didn't! You just read slow!"

At this point Jason and Brianna's mom steps in to break up the argument. Brianna picks up her book, puts it away, and goes outside. Jason's mom is not happy that he knocked his sister's book to the floor. She tells him to go to his room and finish his reading.

Think about this story to answer these questions.

1. Which choice best explains why Jason is angry?

    a. Jason is angry at Brianna because she finished reading before he did.

    a. Jason is angry at himself for being a slower reader.

2. What warning signs of anger could Jason have noticed?

    _____

    _____

    _____

    _____

3. When would have been a good time for Jason to use his BRAKE tool?

    _____

    _____

    _____

    _____

BIG DEAL OR LITTLE DEAL QUESTIONS

1. Is Jason safe?   O Yes   O No

2. Is Jason treating others safely or in the way he wants to be treated?
   O Yes   O No

3. Can Jason ask an adult near him for help?   O Yes   O No

4. What tools could Jason have used before knocking Brianna's book to the floor?

   _____

   _____

5. What might Brianna be thinking?

   _____

   _____

6. Are Jason's feelings so high that it is impossible for him to think clearly?
   O Yes   O No

7. If Jason had not acted on his anger and followed the urge to knock
   Brianna's book down, what might he have done instead?

   _____

   _____

   _____

(See Appendix D for answers.)

MORE

93

MORE FOR YOU TO DO

Practice using the Big Deal or Little Deal questions and keep track of your results. Set a goal of trying to practice once each day for a week and see how you do.

DATE/EVENT	DID I ASK THE BIG DEAL AND LITTLE DEAL QUESTIONS?	WERE THEY HELPFUL?
	O YES O NO	O NO, NOT AT ALL O YES, BUT ONLY A LITTLE O YES, A LOT!
	O YES O NO	O NO, NOT AT ALL O YES, BUT ONLY A LITTLE O YES, A LOT!
	O YES O NO	O NO, NOT AT ALL O YES, BUT ONLY A LITTLE O YES, A LOT!
	O YES O NO	O NO, NOT AT ALL O YES, BUT ONLY A LITTLE O YES, A LOT!
	O YES O NO	O NO, NOT AT ALL O YES, BUT ONLY A LITTLE O YES, A LOT!
	O YES O NO	O NO, NOT AT ALL O YES, BUT ONLY A LITTLE O YES, A LOT!

Talk! Talk! Talk!

FOR YOU TO KNOW

Talking about how you feel is the best way to start to feel better.

When anger sneaks up on you, you may feel like you are about to explode! It's like a balloon with too much air in it. If you don't let some of the air out, the balloon will pop.

People are not the same as balloons, though, so that makes it more difficult. How do people let out some air or blow off some steam? The answer is by talking. Some people have said that when you're angry you should punch a pillow, but this is actually bad advice. Researchers and scientist have learned that doing this actually teaches our brain to be violent or hurt others when we're angry. That's not what we want to teach our brain.

Using your words and finding an adult or friend to listen when you are angry is the best way to let some pressure out and express your anger.

FOR YOU TO DO

Color the illustration below and think about how you can use this tool when you are angry. Some anger words and phrases are listed, and add any words or phrases you think you might use when you're letting out the pressure of anger.

ACTIVITY 32

Riding the Wave of Anger

FOR YOU TO KNOW

Sometimes anger is so big and strong that you can actually feel it in your body, pushing you to do something you don't want to do or wouldn't normally do. You can't stop the anger, but you can try to ride it out, stay strong, and wait for it to pass, like a wave.

Strong feelings are like waves: they can be so big that they knock you over and you get sand in your swimsuit and water up your nose! But if you see the wave coming, you can ride on the top of it with a boogie board or a surfboard. If you see the wave coming, you can dive under it or over it. If you see the wave coming, you can adjust your feet and stand strong until it passes.

The best tool for helping you ride the wave of anger is to focus on your breathing. If you were an actual surfer, you'd have to learn to hold your breath when you go under a wave. With anger, you do the opposite. When you feel anger swelling up, focus on your breathing and wait for the wave of anger to pass. Remember that anger always passes.

The diagrams below can help you practice controlling your breathing. Trace your finger on the figure eight. Place your finger on the star in the center, and take a deep breath in as you trace the right side of the eight. When your finger passes the star again, slowly let your breath out while tracing the left side. Repeat as you trace the symbol.

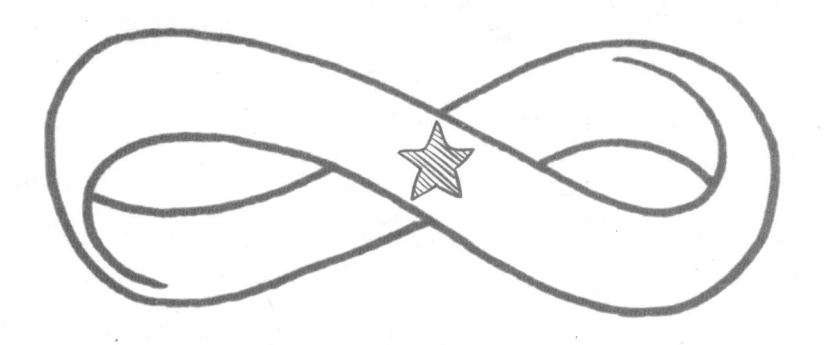

Trace your finger on the square. Start in one corner, and breathe in slowly as you move toward the next corner. At that corner, slowly exhale as you move to the next corner. Continue this pattern as you move around the square, changing your breathing at each corner.

Catch It! Check It! Reverse It!

When your angry feelings are so big that they feel in control of your behaviors, doing the opposite of your first urge can actually change how you feel.

When anger is high, it takes over your brain and urges you to act in a certain way. An urge is a thought about doing something right before you do it. It can be hard to catch your urges before they become actions.

A great trick is to remember these words: "Catch it! Check it! Reverse it!"

- **Catch it!** Use your BRAKE tool to catch your thought or urge *before* you act.

- **Check it!** Take a moment to think about your actions. Is this urge about to get you in more trouble? Will it make you feel bad about yourself once the feeling has passed?

- **Reverse it!** If you can't change your thoughts, do the opposite of what your urge is telling you to do.

Draw a line from the feeling you might have to the urge and then to the reverse action you could do to change your feeling. You can use the blank lines to add other feelings, urges, or reverse actions to this chart.

CATCH IT! What am I feeling?	CHECK IT! What is my urge?	REVERSE IT! What can I do instead?
ANGRY	SCREAM!	BREATHE DEEPLY
FRUSTRATED	YELL!	WHISPER
ANNOYED	CALL NAMES!	USE KIND WORDS
IRRITATED	USE MEAN WORDS!	SAY NOTHING
MAD	HIT!	SHAKE IT OUT
	KICK!	WALK AWAY
	BREAK THINGS!	

Try to Catch It! Check It! Reverse It! and see how it feels. It might feel weird at first, but stick with it and it will start to feel normal.

When Anger Keeps Happening

FOR YOU TO KNOW

Problem solving is a tool you can use to change situations that keep happening over and over and lead to anger outbursts or poor choices.

Sometimes no matter how hard you try to use your tools and control your anger, things still don't go your way. That can be very frustrating and make your anger grow bigger. When it happens, you might need to problem solve so that you can reduce the chances of the same thing happening again.

Read through these six steps of problem solving:

1. Describe the problem. What caused your anger?

2. What would make you feel better? What is your goal? Make sure that this is something you actually have control over. Remember, you can never control the actions of others; you can control only yourself.

3. Brainstorm a list of ideas to reach your goal. Any idea may turn out to be the one that works!

4. Choose what you think is the best idea. If you are not sure, choose two ideas to compare. Keep your list; you might need to come back to it.

5. Try it out! Put your plan into action. If you think you might need help, ask a trusted adult.

6. Evaluate. Did your idea work? Does the new outcome make you feel better about the situation?

   a. Yes? Great job! You've problem solved the situation that caused the anger.

   b. No? Go back to your list of ideas and try another one. You'll get it. Sometimes it takes time and lots of tries to get it right.

Use this worksheet to write out your problem-solving steps. For each step, an example has been provided. At http://www.newharbinger.com/47278, you can download a blank worksheet for more practice.

1. Describe the problem. What caused your anger?

   I hate riding the bus to school in the morning because the kid who sits behind me kicks my seat. That makes me mad, and I end up getting in trouble.

   _____

   _____

   _____

   _____

2. What would make you feel better? What is your goal?

   I would feel better if I could get to school without already being in trouble.

   _____

   _____

   _____

   _____

MORE ➤

3. Brainstorm a list of ideas. Any idea may turn out to be the one that works!

Walk to school. Ask Mom to drive me. Put a magic spell on the kid behind me to stop kicking my seat. Talk to the bus driver about switching seats. Ask the bus driver to help keep me and the other kid separated.

_____

_____

_____

_____

4. Choose what you think is the best idea. If you are not sure, choose two ideas to compare.

Compare two ideas: 1. Ask Mom to drive me and 2. Ask bus driver to keep us separate. Mom can't give me a ride, so I'll try talking to the bus driver.

_____

_____

_____

_____

5. Try it out! Put your plan into action. What did you do?

_____

_____

_____

_____

6. Evaluate. Did your idea work? Does the new outcome make you feel better about the situation?

_____

_____

_____

_____

a. Yes? Great job! You've problem solved the situation that caused the anger.

b. No? Go back to your list of ideas and try another one. You'll get it. Sometimes it takes time and lots of tries to get it right.

ACTIVITY
35

Putting It All Together

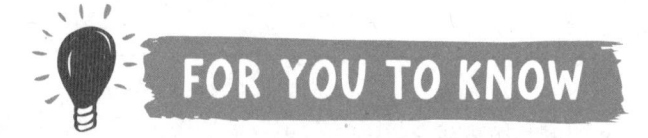

FOR YOU TO KNOW

It takes up to two months to really learn and become good at a new behavior.

We have covered a lot in this workbook. We learned about identifying anger and how quickly it can take over. We learned about the things that feed it and make it bigger, and we learned about different ways to slow it down. Now what you need to do is practice using these skills in your daily life. This means you need to think about them throughout the day, not only when you are looking at this workbook.

FOR YOU TO DO

Use this worksheet to practice your new skills over and over and over again. You can download it at http://www.newharbinger.com/47278. Make as many copies as you need to practice.

What happened? <u>Jesse took the ball.</u>

1. CATCH IT!
- **Use BRAKE tool**

Am I seeing all sides? Am I in Full Mind, Fact Mind, Feeling Mind? <u>Fact: Jesse took the ball.</u> Is this a big deal or a little deal? <u>Little deal.</u>

2. CHECK IT!
- *Slow it down*
- *Big deal/little deal*

repeat as needed

Can I change my thoughts to change my anger? <u>Wait it out: take a few deep breaths.</u> Can I reverse it? Can I do the opposite? <u>Reverse it: share.</u>

3. CHANGE IT!
- *Talk*
- *Wait it out*

OR **REVERSE IT!**
- *Brake*
- *Do the opposite*

Is there a middle path? <u>Play together.</u> Do I need to problem solve? <u>Make a plan to play together.</u> What can I do to refuel?

4. RETURN TO FULL MIND
- *Middle path*
- *Problem solve*
- *Refuel*

APPENDIX A: For Parents

Section 1: Feelings and Thoughts

This section provides a general introduction to the various feelings we experience and the concept that feelings come in different sizes, or intensities. This is not a section focused on change; that comes later in the book. These activities are meant to help you get a sense of your child's existing understanding of emotions and what might cause them. The section introduces the reader to the idea that we have feelings for a reason. It is important for kids to learn that their feelings can be helpful, even when they are uncomfortable.

Activity 5 in this section covers a very important concept. This activity introduces the reader to three states of mind: feeling mind, fact mind, and full mind. The most important of these for children to understand is *feeling mind*. This is the state of mind where our actions are driven by emotions, regardless of the facts. We are impulsive, say and do things we don't mean, and do things that tend to get us in trouble. This state of mind, which happens to both kids and adults, is temporary, even though at the time we tend to think it will last forever. Helping your child recognize when this happens to them, and what their warning signs are, can help them feel more in control. Thinking about the facts of the situation—*fact mind*—can help pull them from feeling mind into the middle ground, full mind. *Full mind* is a combination of both feelings and facts. This does not mean that full mind is not uncomfortable. It can be, because it still includes feelings, specifically in this book, anger.

➡️ HOW CAN YOU HELP?

Focus on getting a sense of what your child does and does not know about feelings. This section is not about change. Fight the urge to give directives for change at this point. Listen and explore.

If your child is struggling to answer some of the questions or to think about how these concepts apply to themself, use yourself as an example. It's important for kids to know that adults have these same feelings and experiences. They are more likely to open up if they know they are not alone in the struggle.

Section 2: Focusing on Understanding Anger

This section is where we begin to focus specifically on anger. There are a few concepts in this section that intentionally have repeated activities. Having kids approach and practice these concepts from different angles will help them fully understand and practice their new skills. In this section, we learn about what triggers anger, both in general and also personally. Many kids who struggle with intense anger are not able to notice their anger until it is at such a high intensity that it has already crossed over to uncontrollable. There are a few activities in this section that encourage kids to identify how anger feels in their body, connecting their sensations with their actions. One of the goals here is for kids to identify and catch the anger before it is out of control. By catching the anger at a lower intensity, and then changing their thoughts or actions, they have a better chance at regaining control.

Another key takeaway from this section is slowing things down. In Activity 15, children are encouraged to learn the difference between thoughts, urges, and behaviors. In Activity 16, they practice breaking down the parts of big emotions and the events that lead to them. Intense anger sneaks up on kids very quickly. We want to teach them to slow down and wait for the anger to pass—it always does. By slowing down, they will feel more mastery and control.

➡ HOW CAN YOU HELP?

There are a few activities in this section that talk about thoughts and urges. You can help your child by sharing some of your own thoughts or urges out loud, like a sports announcer giving a play-by-play. This may feel odd, but it's a great way to model this process for kids. They learn from watching the adults around them.

Section 3: Anger Can Hurt Others

Section 3 encourages kids to think about how anger impacts their interactions with others and what others think of them. Activity 20 uses a sandcastle metaphor to demonstrate to the reader that repeated actions of anger can slowly destroy friendships. It is important for kids to learn that how they treat others determines whether others want to spend time with them or be their friend.

This section also asks kids to think about values, or what kind of person they want to be. This serves two purposes. First, identifying what kind of person they want to be and what values are important to them will increase their sense of self. Second, the reader is asked to identify behaviors, or actions, connected to those values. The objective is to help kids put their values into action. When you feel good about your actions, you feel good about yourself.

Activity 24 encourages the reader to find the middle path. This requires increased flexibility and might be hard for some kids, especially when their anger is high. They will need help and practice with this. You may want to start with situations with smaller intensity.

 **HOW CAN YOU HELP?**

Take the time to talk through these concepts with your child. Relationships are hard for both children and adults. These concepts will take time and repetition.

If you notice that your child's peers are not responding well to them due to their anger actions, talk to your child about it. It's never too early for them to learn that their actions have an impact on those around them and carry potential consequences.

Section 4: Pushing Back Against Anger

This section is when we finally focus on changing anger actions. Often, adults move too quickly past understanding and validating how their children feel. They tend to move straight into directions—what to do or how to correct the behavior right away. Slow down. Once children feel understood, they are more open to change. Many adults are afraid that by slowing down and acknowledging, or validating, a child's intense emotions they are approving the related actions. This is not the case. You can validate an intense emotion and not validate an inappropriate or dangerous behavior.

The skills in this book are not rocket science! The trick is to encourage your child to use them purposefully when anger becomes intense and out of control. Activity 29 provides an opportunity to involve the entire family in practicing their skills. Use the tokens in Activity 29 to catch all family members making observable changes to behavior.

In Activity 34, kids walk through the steps of problem solving. This can potentially be overwhelming, as it has many steps involved. However, each step is important. When the same situations that prompt anger keep happening over and over, your child may need to problem solve in order to see lasting change.

Finally, Activity 35 puts all of these concepts together in a model for emotions and skill use. This page is reproducible. Make several copies for your child. This takes practice, practice, practice! You can even fill one out yourself to model for your child how it works.

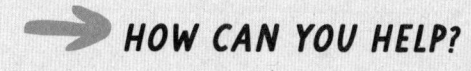 **HOW CAN YOU HELP?**

Use these skills yourself and model them for your child. Kids learn most through experiences and watching those around them. Just doing the worksheets is not enough.

APPENDIX B: Anger Control Cheat Sheet

When you are really, really angry, it can be hard to remember what you've been practicing. This cheat sheet lists all the skills you've learned about in this book. Seeing them written out in front of you can help you remember which ones to try.

Download the Anger Control Cheat Sheet at http://www.newharbinger.com /47278, and make enough copies to post in your room and around your house.

ANGER CONTROL CHEAT SHEET

FULL MIND	Make a wise decision by focusing on both the facts of the situation and your feelings.
CATCH IT!	Stop and notice what is going on inside and outside of you. How are you feeling? Where do you feel it in your body? How big is your feeling?
CHECK IT!	Check all the information you have. Are you looking at all sides of the story, or are you focusing only on your feeling thoughts?
CHANGE IT!	Change your thoughts on purpose. Focus your thinking on something else until your anger gets smaller.
SLOW IT DOWN	Anger sneaks up on you very fast and can feel like it takes over. Slow down on purpose to stay in control.
WAIT IT OUT	Anger does not last forever. Wait for the anger to pass before acting.
RIDE THE WAVE	When it makes sense to be angry, feel your anger come and go in your body like a wave. Control your breath to control your anger.
MAKE A DEAL	Look for a way to help each person feel better about the situation. You may need to compromise.
BRAKE	Take a deep **BREATH**. **RELAX** your muscles. **ASK** about the facts/**ASK** for help. Be **KIND** to yourself and others. **ENTER** the situation when ready.
BIG DEAL OR LITTLE DEAL?	Ask yourself: Am I safe? Am I treating others safely or the way I want to be treated? Can I ask an adult near me for help? Have I used my tools before acting? Can I put myself in the other person's shoes? What might they be thinking or feeling? Are my feelings too high, making it impossible for me to think clearly? Have I waited for my anger to pass before choosing my actions?
TALK!	Talk it out with a trusted friend or adult. Use your words to express your anger, and let some of the anger out.
REFUEL	Refuel your strength against anger by doing something positive on purpose to increase your positive feelings and decrease your anger.
REVERSE IT!	Use your **BRAKE** to catch it and check it. If you can't change your thought, reverse it and do the opposite of your urge.
PROBLEM SOLVING	When you notice that the same frustrating situations happen over and over, go through the problem-solving steps to make a change.

APPENDIX C: How Big Is Your Feeling?
An Interactive Game for Practicing Your Skills

Learning new skills and changing behavior takes a lot of practice. How Big Is Your Feeling? is a game to help you practice identifying your feelings and how big, or intense, they are in different situations. You can play with friends, siblings, and even your parents. Parents need to practice these skills too!

This game includes a Feelings Pack, which helps you practice getting to know all the basic feelings; an Anger Pack, which focuses on getting to know your anger better; and an Anger Control Pack, which covers the skills you learned in this book. Think of the Anger Control Pack as bonus cards. You can use them with the other two packs to practice the skills you would use in each situation.

Download the cards at http://www.newharbinger.com/47278 or photocopy them from the next few pages. There are blank cards included for you to add any feelings or skills that may not be listed. There are also blank situation cards to add if you would like.

You can play this game with any number of players. During the game, talk with the other player(s) about why they chose the feeling and intensity they did. Having different feelings and different feeling intensities is not good or bad, right or wrong; it's just different. Most people have more than one feeling at a time, so use as many cards as you think you might need.

Have fun and be creative! The goal is to get more comfortable with your anger and practice using the skills you've learned in this workbook.

Card Packs

- **FEELINGS PACK — Feeling Cards**
- **FEELINGS PACK — Situation Cards**
- **ANGER PACK — Feeling Cards**
- **ANGER PACK — Situation Cards**
- **ANGER CONTROL CARDS**
- **INTENSITY CARDS**

How to Play

1. Deal each player a set of feeling cards, one of each feeling, and a set of intensity cards, one of each number.

2. Place the situation cards facedown in the middle of the table.

3. The first player picks a situation card from the pile in the middle and reads the situation out loud.

4. Every player chooses the feeling or feelings they would have in that situation, and the number that represents the intensity, or size, of the feeling. Talk about any differences or similarities among the players.

5. The game continues until all the situation cards have been turned over and talked about.

Remember that everyone might have a different feeling and intensity. This is a normal part of having feelings! Different does not mean wrong; it just means different.

Other Ways to Play

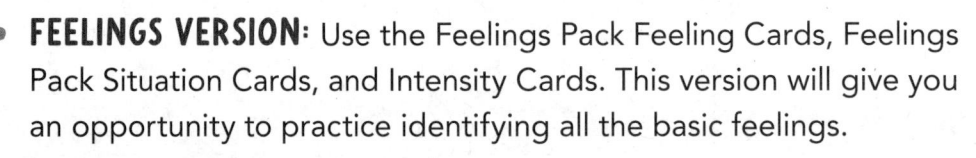

- **FEELINGS VERSION:** Use the Feelings Pack Feeling Cards, Feelings Pack Situation Cards, and Intensity Cards. This version will give you an opportunity to practice identifying all the basic feelings.

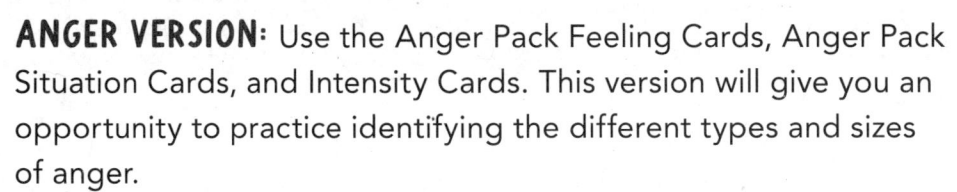

- **ANGER VERSION:** Use the Anger Pack Feeling Cards, Anger Pack Situation Cards, and Intensity Cards. This version will give you an opportunity to practice identifying the different types and sizes of anger.

- **USING THE ANGER CONTROL CARDS:** Follow the general game instructions, and also give each player a set of Anger Control Cards. As you play, each player puts down the anger control skills they would use or think about in each situation. Remember, it's best to use as many skills as you need to be successful in managing anger.

You could also play a version that includes all the feelings and situation cards at the same time.

Download the cards at
http://www.newharbinger.com/47278
or photocopy them from the next few pages.

FEELINGS PACK — Feelings Cards

Anger	Fear	Jealousy
Guilt	Overwhelmed Excited	Love
Sadness	Happiness Joy	_____

FEELINGS PACK — Situation Cards

YOUR BROTHER TAKES YOUR FAVORITE TOY.	SOMEONE AT SCHOOL TAKES YOUR PLACE IN LINE.	YOUR SISTER CALLS YOU A NAME.
THE FAMILY PLANS CHANGE! YOU CAN'T GO TO THE ZOO (OR YOUR FAVORITE PLACE).	YOUR CLASSMATE IS SITTING TOO CLOSE TO YOU.	YOU LOSE YOUR FAVORITE TOY OR SPECIAL ITEM.
YOU LOSE A GAME.	YOU BLAME YOUR SISTER FOR SOMETHING AND SHE GETS IN TROUBLE.	YOU WANT TO TELL YOUR MOM A STORY, AND SHE IS BUSY LISTENING TO YOUR BROTHER.

YOU GET EXACTLY WHAT YOU ASKED FOR YOUR BIRTHDAY.	YOUR BROTHER GETS YOUR FAVORITE THING FOR HIS BIRTHDAY.	A FRIEND AT SCHOOL TEASES YOU.
YOU ARE MEETING YOUR NEW TEACHER FOR THE FIRST TIME.	YOU HAVE TO GIVE A PRESENTATION IN FRONT OF THE CLASS.	YOU HAVE TO TAKE A TEST.
YOU'RE AT A BIRTHDAY PARTY AND EVERYONE IS HAVING THE BEST TIME EVER!	YOU AND YOUR BROTHER ARE RUNNING AROUND PLAYING YOUR FAVORITE GAME. IT IS SO EXCITING!	YOU ARE LEFT OUT OF A GAME AT SCHOOL.

ANGER PACK — Feeling Cards

Angry	Annoyed	Irritated
Fuming	Irked	Furious
Outraged	Livid	Frustrated

Aggravated	Grouchy	Agitated
Bitter	Grumpy	Cranky

ANGER PACK — Situation Cards

Your sister gets the latest iPhone as a birthday gift, and you've been asking for it forever.	You've worked on your science Project for two weeks. The day of the science fair you are carrying it into school. You drop it and it falls apart.	The boy who sits next to you hums during class. It's not super loud, but you can hear it and it makes it hard for you to concentrate.
You're in the family room playing your favorite video game with your best friend. Your sister comes in and insists on sitting near you while she's talking on the phone.	You have a hard time sleeping and are awake most of the night. The next morning, your mom wakes you up extra early.	You have a bit of a cold and still have to go to school. You're not super sick but you don't want to be at school yet.
You're walking through the cafeteria when someone trips you and you fall down. Everyone starts to laugh.	On Monday, you got into a small disagreement with your best friend. On Tuesday, you notice that you are having a hard time wanting to interact with them.	You are given homework that you don't understand. You sit and stare at the worksheet for Ten minutes until you start to feel a pit in your stomach and your face turns red.

ANGER PACK — Situation Cards
continued

The teacher is making some morning announcements. The kid behind you punches you in the back. You try to tell the teacher, who just says, "Be quiet and listen."	You're excited about a friend's birthday party coming up, but then she tells you she is allowed to invite only four people—and you are not one of them.	You're playing a video game when your mom gets home from work. She turns off the power and tells you to start your homework—even though you don't even have any. All your progress in the game is lost.
You and your best friend have an argument. Your friend starts spending a lot of time with someone you don't like. One day your friend's new buddy tells you they are a better friend than you could ever be.	Lately your parents have been fighting a lot. Your older brother says it's your fault and the whole family would have been a lot better off if you were never born.	A teacher accuses you of cheating on a test you aced. When you are trying to defend yourself, the teacher says there is no way you could have gotten all the right answers on your own.
Someone you thought was a friend spreads a rumor about you. At lunch, you see the person sitting with a bunch of your friends. They're all looking at you and laughing.	You and your brother are in the family room, and your mom is in the kitchen. She overhears someone say a curse word. She thinks it was you when it was actually your brother, and you end up getting in trouble.	Your parents are divorced and it's supposed to be your weekend at your dad's house. He tells you he is going out of town so you have to spend the weekend at your mom's and you have to pack right away.

Anger Control Cards

Full Mind	Catch It!	Check It!
Change It!	Slow It Down	Wait It Out
Ride the Wave	Make a Deal	Refuel

Anger Control Cards *continued*

BRAKE	Big Deal or Little Deal?	Talk
Reverse It!	Problem Solve	________

Intensity Cards

1	2	3

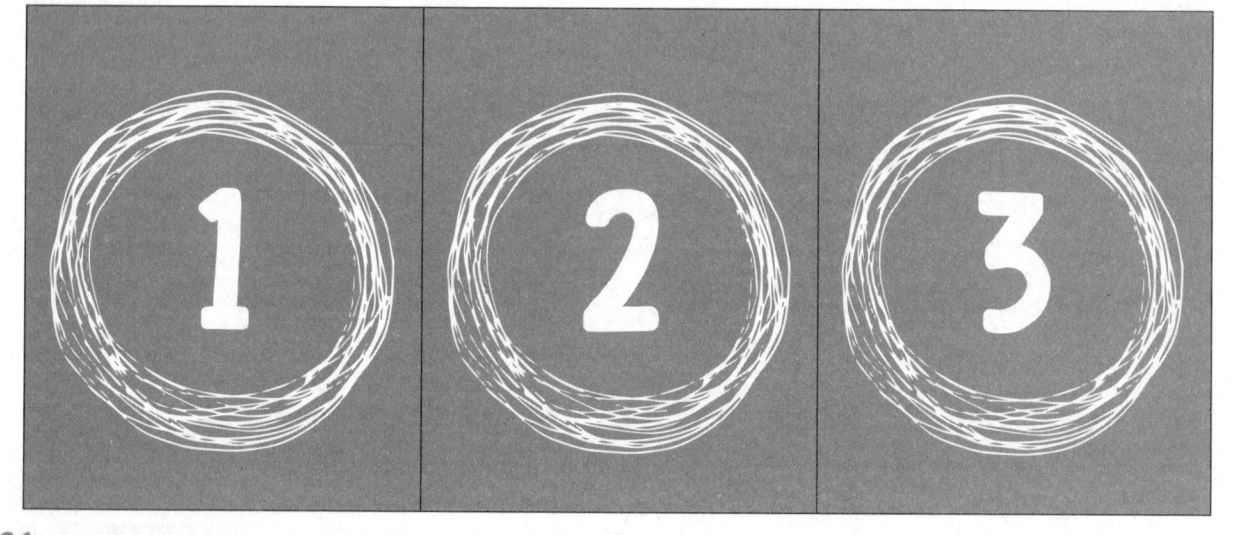

Appendix D: Activity Answers

Activity 1

1. happy, excited; 2. happy, excited, nervous, anxious; 3. sad, disappointed, mad, angry; 4. angry, mad, jealous; 5. guilty; 6. anxious, nervous; 7. sad

Activity 4

1. run, get out of here!; 2. fear; 3. look; 4. run!

Activity 4 (More for You to Do)

1. Something is wrong. There's danger; 2. The tiger in the room; 3. Run out of the room and to safety.

Activity 8 (Word Search)

A	I	N	D	I	G	N	A	N	T	I	U	I	D
U	U	D	E	G	A	R	T	U	O	E	T	G	F
T	A	N	V	A	U	V	S	D	R	X	F	I	I
L	T	D	T	T	D	E	A	I	Y	A	R	R	E
U	G	R	A	G	I	N	G	R	H	S	U	R	R
F	G	S	R	E	A	G	I	R	C	P	S	I	C
H	O	S	T	I	L	E	T	I	U	E	T	T	E
T	Y	R	P	G	P	F	A	T	O	R	R	A	I
A	E	O	I	E	E	U	T	A	R	A	A	T	N
R	Y	R	G	N	A	L	E	B	G	T	T	E	G
W	B	I	T	T	E	R	D	L	A	E	E	D	M
G	R	U	M	P	Y	N	R	E	R	D	D	I	A
H	D	E	T	A	V	A	R	G	G	A	B	T	D
A	N	N	O	Y	E	D	S	U	O	I	R	U	F

Activity 10

Circle: never, hate, always, no way, forever, forget it, absolutely not, every time, constantly, refuse, revenge, unending

Underline: truce, kindness, help, deal, sympathy, trust, compromise, middle path, respect, negotiate, calm, patient

Activity 11

Underline: I can't believe we lost.   We should have won.   The other team should not have won! They suck!   I hate that we lost.   We should have won.

Circle: We did the best we could.   We'll beat 'em next time.   We'll play again tomorrow.

Activity 17

"This goal is important to me. I need to problem solve."

"This person is being mean. I need to let them know I don't like what is happening."

"I lost the game! I need to practice more. I can get better and win next time."

"I don't like what's happening. I need to get an adult's help."

Activity 24

1. b or d; 2. b or c; 3. c

Activity 30

1. b (Jason's anger originates from his frustration with himself. His sister has not actually done anything to Jason.)

2. His muscles were tightening up and his breathing was changing.

3. Jason could have used his BRAKE skill as soon as he noticed the anger in his body.

Activity 30 (Big Deal or Little Deal Questions)

1. Yes

2. No

3. Yes (He could talk to his parent about needing help in reading.)

4. Deep breathing; Ask his fact mind, *Has Brianna done something to me to deserve my anger?*

5. *Why is Jason mad at me? What did I do to him?*

6. Yes

7. Use his skills to calm his anger; Ask his mom for help with his reading; Talk to his teacher about how hard reading is for him.

Christina Kress, MSW, LICSW, is a licensed clinical social worker in private practice near Minneapolis, MN. Kress has eighteen years of experience treating children and families using play therapy and cognitive behavioral therapy (CBT), along with ten years of experience treating adults and teens using dialectical behavior therapy (DBT). Kress presents annually at the Minnesota Association for Child and Adolescent Mental Health Conference; has been a guest lecturer at St. Catherine's University in St. Paul, MN; and provides clinical supervision to mental health practitioners through her practice.

More ⏱ Instant Help Books for Kids

An Imprint of New Harbinger Publications

THE RELAXATION AND STRESS REDUCTION WORKBOOK FOR KIDS

Help for Children to Cope with Stress, Anxiety, and Transitions

978-1572245822 / US $21.95

THE ANXIETY WORKBOOK FOR KIDS

Take Charge of Fears and Worries Using the Gift of Imagination

978-1626254770 / US $18.95

MASTER OF MINDFULNESS

How to Be Your Own Superhero in Times of Stress

978-1626254640 / US $14.95

THE ADHD WORKBOOK FOR KIDS

Helping Children Gain Self-Confidence, Social Skills, and Self-Control

978-1572247666 / US $17.95

DON'T LET YOUR EMOTIONS RUN YOUR LIFE FOR KIDS

A DBT-Based Skills Workbook to Help Children Manage Mood Swings, Control Angry Outbursts, and Get Along with Others

978-1626258594 / US $18.95

RAISING GOOD HUMANS

A Mindful Guide to Breaking the Cycle of Reactive Parenting and Raising Kind, Confident Kids

978-1684033881 / US $16.95

🌱 newharbingerpublications

1-800-748-6273 / newharbinger.com

(VISA, MC, AMEX / prices subject to change without notice)

Follow Us 📷 f 🐦 ▶ 📌 in

Don't miss out on new books in the subjects that interest you.
Sign up for our Book Alerts at **newharbinger.com/bookalerts** 🖱

Did you know there are free tools you can download for this book?

Free tools are things like **worksheets**, **guided meditation exercises**, and **more** that will help you get the most out of your book.

You can download free tools for this book—whether you bought or borrowed it, in any format, from any source—from the **New Harbinger** website. All you need is a NewHarbinger.com account. Just use the URL provided in this book to view the free tools that are available for it. Then, click on the "download" button for the free tool you want, and follow the prompts that appear to log in to your NewHarbinger.com account and download the material.

You can also save the free tools for this book to your **Free Tools Library** so you can access them again anytime, just by logging in to your account! Just look for this button on the book's free tools page:

+ save this to my
free tools library

If you need help accessing or downloading free tools, visit **newharbinger.com/faq** or contact us at customerservice@newharbinger.com.

CELEBRATING
40 YEARS